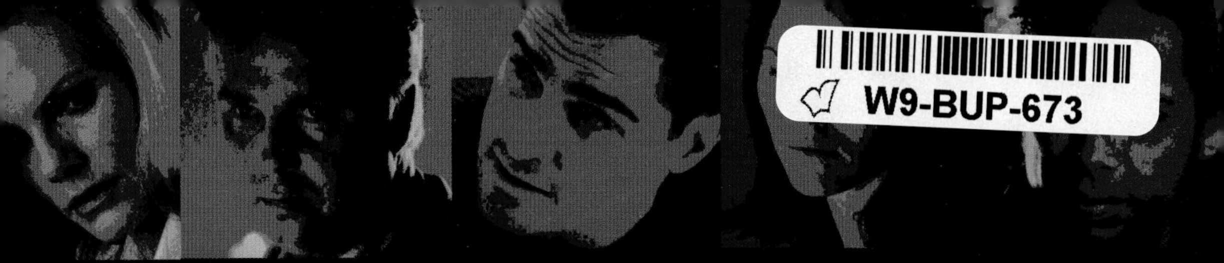

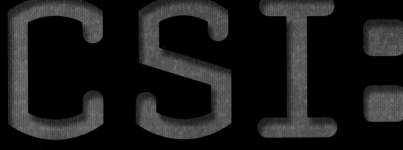

CSI: CRIME SCENE INVESTIGATION™

Demon House

WRITTEN BY MAX ALLAN COLLINS
ART BY GABRIEL RODRIGUEZ
AND ASHLEY WOOD

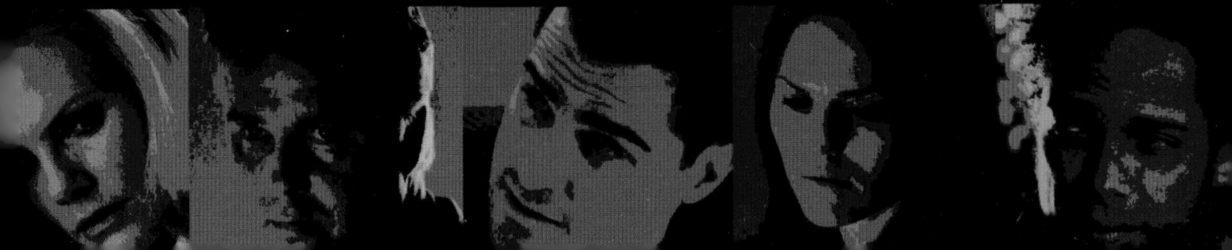

www.idwpublishing.com

ISBN: 1-932382-34-8
07 06 05 04   1 2 3 4 5

Special thanks to Maryann Martin and Ken Ross at
CBS Consumer Products for their invaluable assistance.

CSI: Crime Scene Investigation
Created by Anthony E. Zuiker

Licensed to IDW by CBS Consumer Products

"Demon House"

Written by
Max Allen Collins

Forensics Research/Plot Assist by
Matthew V. Clemens

Pencils and Inks by
Gabriel Rodriguez
Sulaco Studios

Colors by
Frank Gamboa
Sulaco Studios

Lettering and Design by
Robbie Robbins and Cindy Chapman

Original Series Editor: **Jeff Mariotte**

Editor: **Alex Garner**

Cover Photos by
CBS Photo/Robert Voets

Book Design by
Cindy Chapman

Cover Design by
Robbie Robbins

IDW Publishing is:
Ted Adams, Publisher
Chris Ryall, Editor-in-Chief
Robbie Robbins, Design Director
Kris Oprisko, Vice President
Alex Garner, Art Director
Cindy Chapman, Designer
Beau Smith, Sales & Marketing
Chance Boren, Editorial Assistant
Jeremy Corps, Editorial Assistant
Yumiko Miyano, Business Development
Rick Privman, Business Development

Chapter 1

"Fright Night"

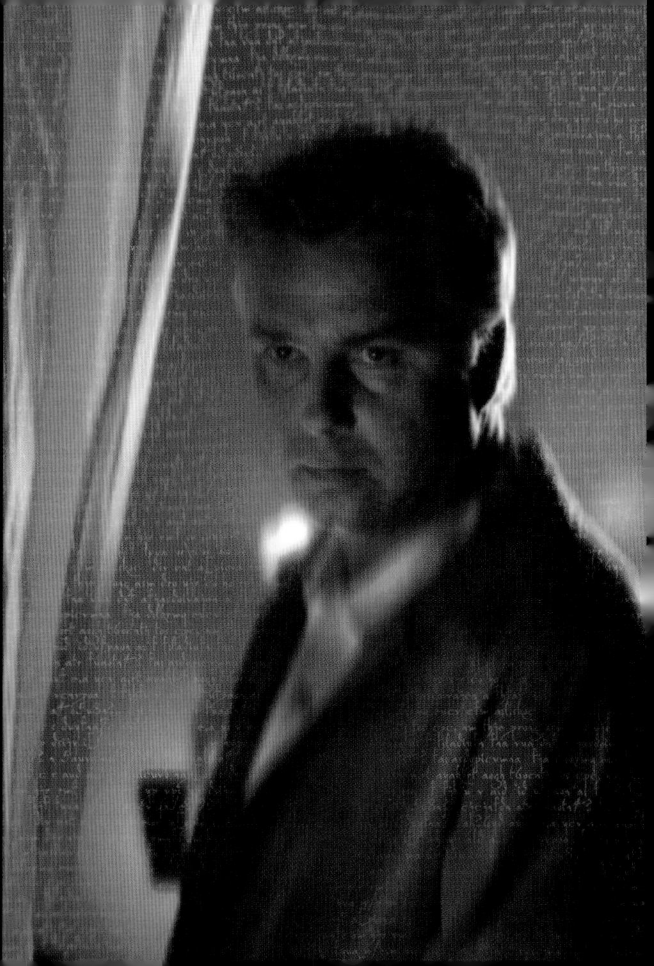

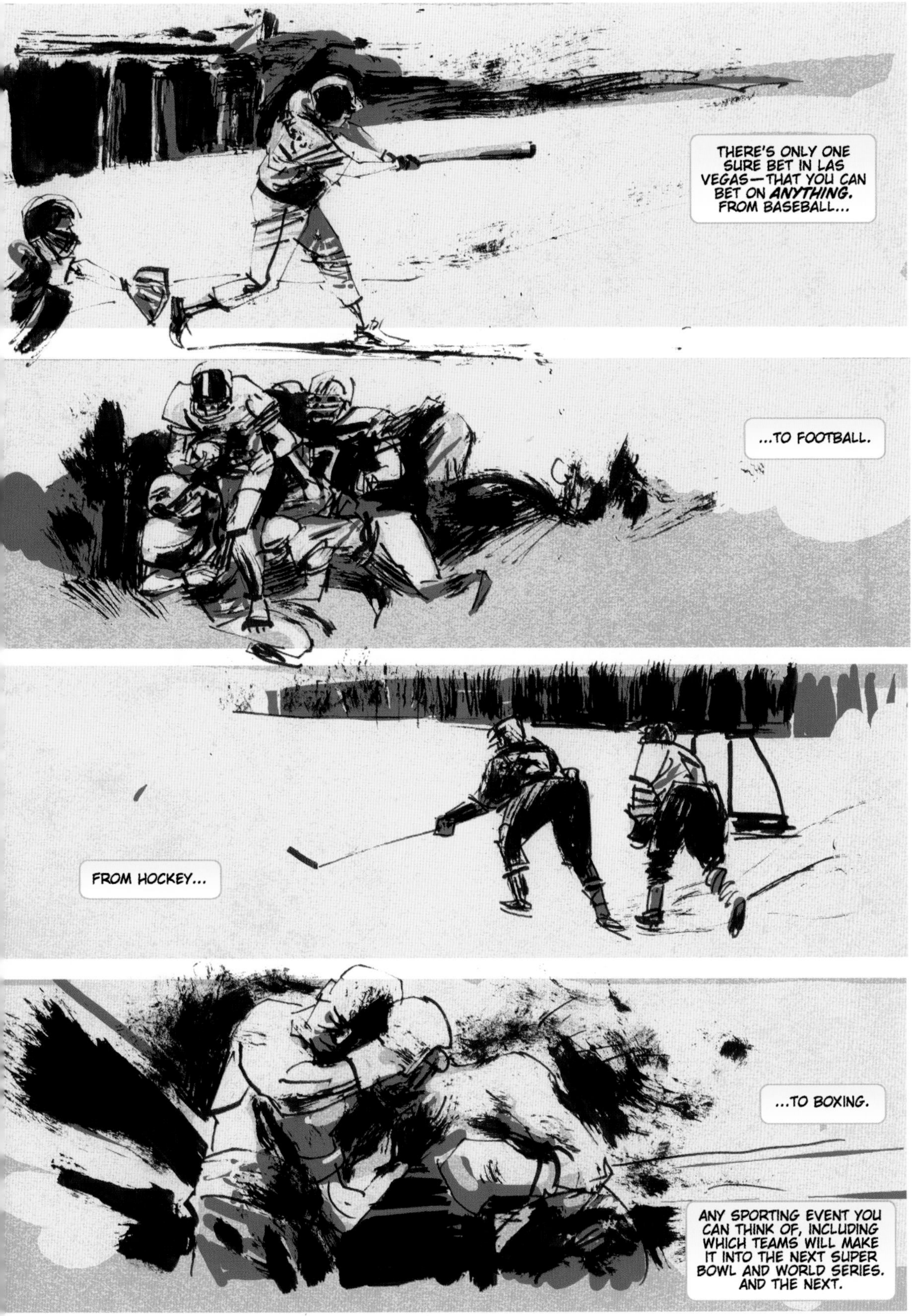

THERE'S ONLY ONE SURE BET IN LAS VEGAS—THAT YOU CAN BET ON *ANYTHING.* FROM BASEBALL...
...TO FOOTBALL.
FROM HOCKEY...
...TO BOXING.
ANY SPORTING EVENT YOU CAN THINK OF, INCLUDING WHICH TEAMS WILL MAKE IT INTO THE NEXT SUPER BOWL AND WORLD SERIES. AND THE NEXT.

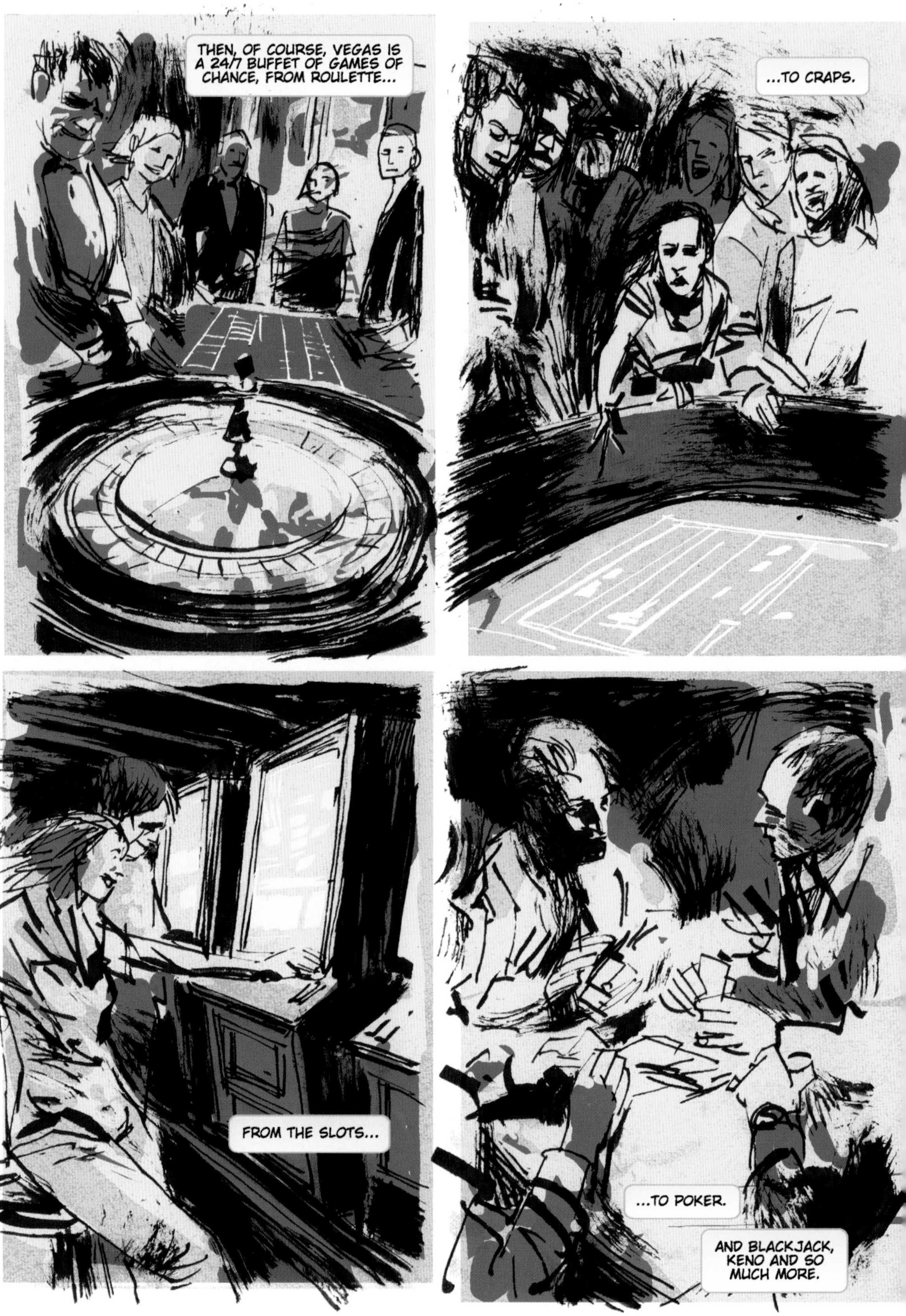
THEN, OF COURSE, VEGAS IS A 24/7 BUFFET OF GAMES OF CHANCE, FROM ROULETTE...
...TO CRAPS.
FROM THE SLOTS...
...TO POKER.
AND BLACKJACK, KENO AND SO MUCH MORE.

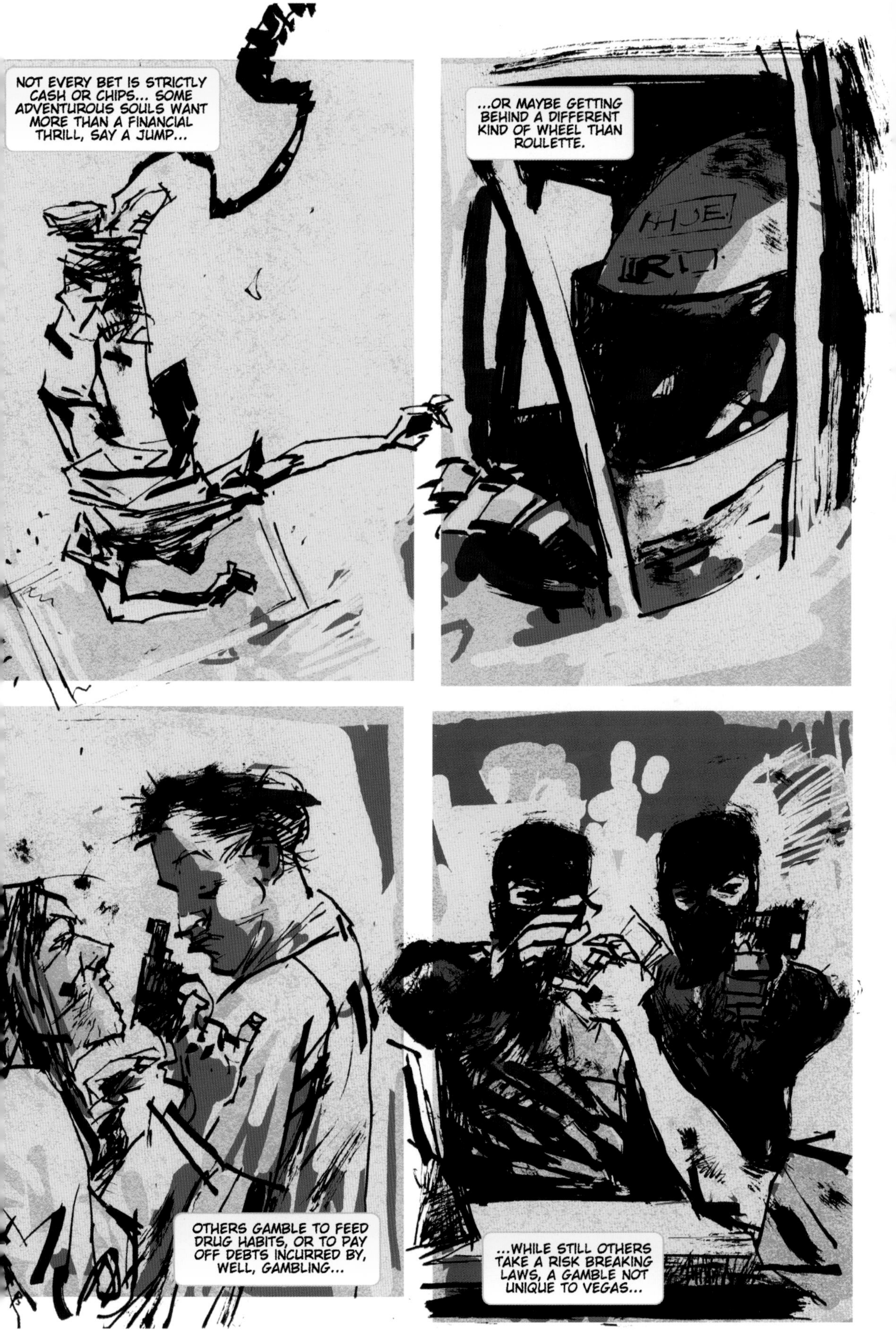
NOT EVERY BET IS STRICTLY CASH OR CHIPS... SOME ADVENTUROUS SOULS WANT MORE THAN A FINANCIAL THRILL, SAY A JUMP...
...OR MAYBE GETTING BEHIND A DIFFERENT KIND OF WHEEL THAN ROULETTE.
OTHERS GAMBLE TO FEED DRUG HABITS, OR TO PAY OFF DEBTS INCURRED BY, WELL, GAMBLING...
...WHILE STILL OTHERS TAKE A RISK BREAKING LAWS, A GAMBLE NOT UNIQUE TO VEGAS...

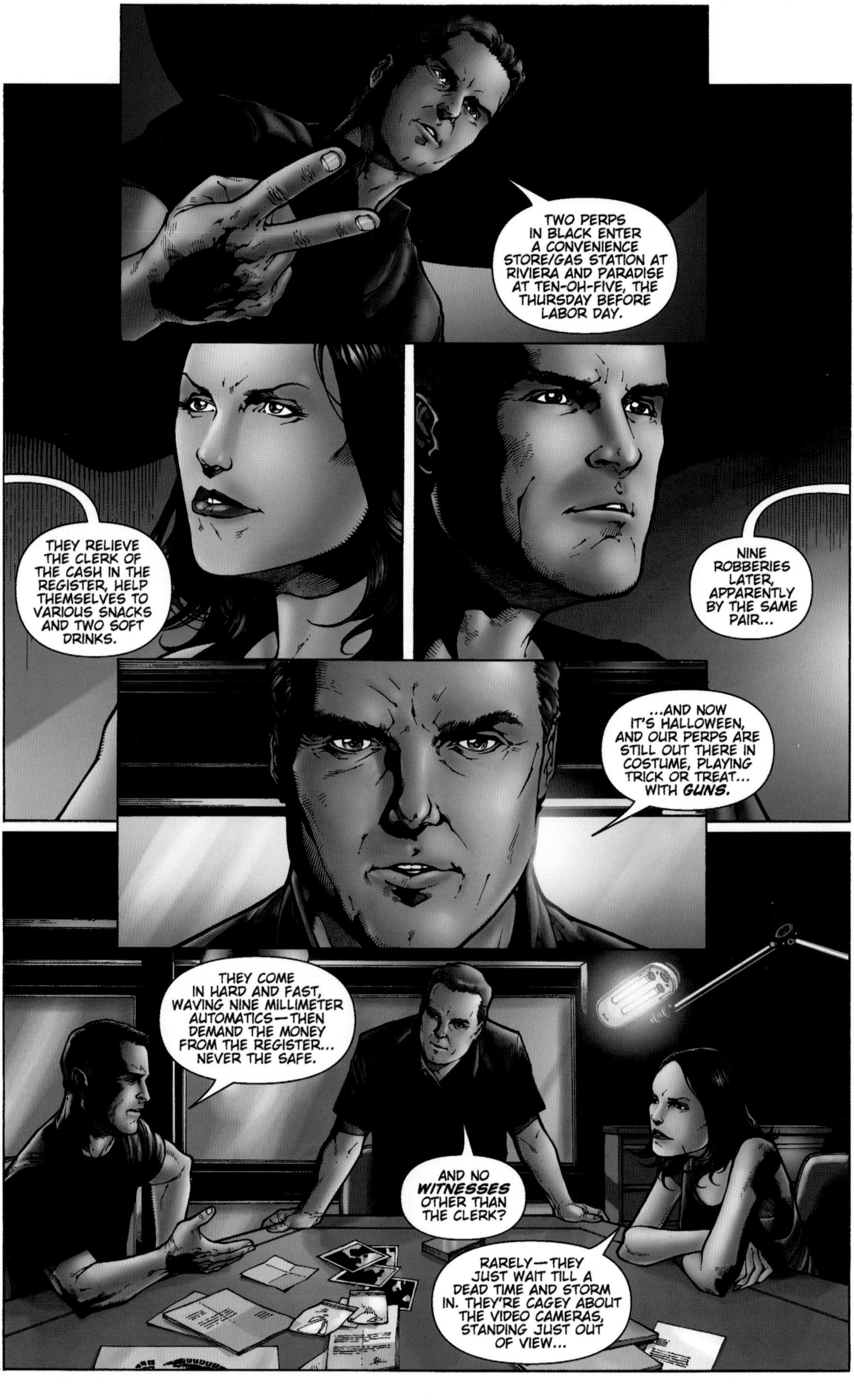
TWO PERPS IN BLACK ENTER A CONVENIENCE STORE/GAS STATION AT RIVIERA AND PARADISE AT TEN-OH-FIVE, THE THURSDAY BEFORE LABOR DAY.
THEY RELIEVE THE CLERK OF THE CASH IN THE REGISTER, HELP THEMSELVES TO VARIOUS SNACKS AND TWO SOFT DRINKS.
NINE ROBBERIES LATER, APPARENTLY BY THE SAME PAIR...
...AND NOW IT'S HALLOWEEN, AND OUR PERPS ARE STILL OUT THERE IN COSTUME, PLAYING TRICK OR TREAT... WITH *GUNS.*
THEY COME IN HARD AND FAST, WAVING NINE MILLIMETER AUTOMATICS—THEN DEMAND THE MONEY FROM THE REGISTER... NEVER THE SAFE.
AND NO *WITNESSES* OTHER THAN THE CLERK?
RARELY—THEY JUST WAIT TILL A DEAD TIME AND STORM IN. THEY'RE CAGEY ABOUT THE VIDEO CAMERAS, STANDING JUST OUT OF VIEW...

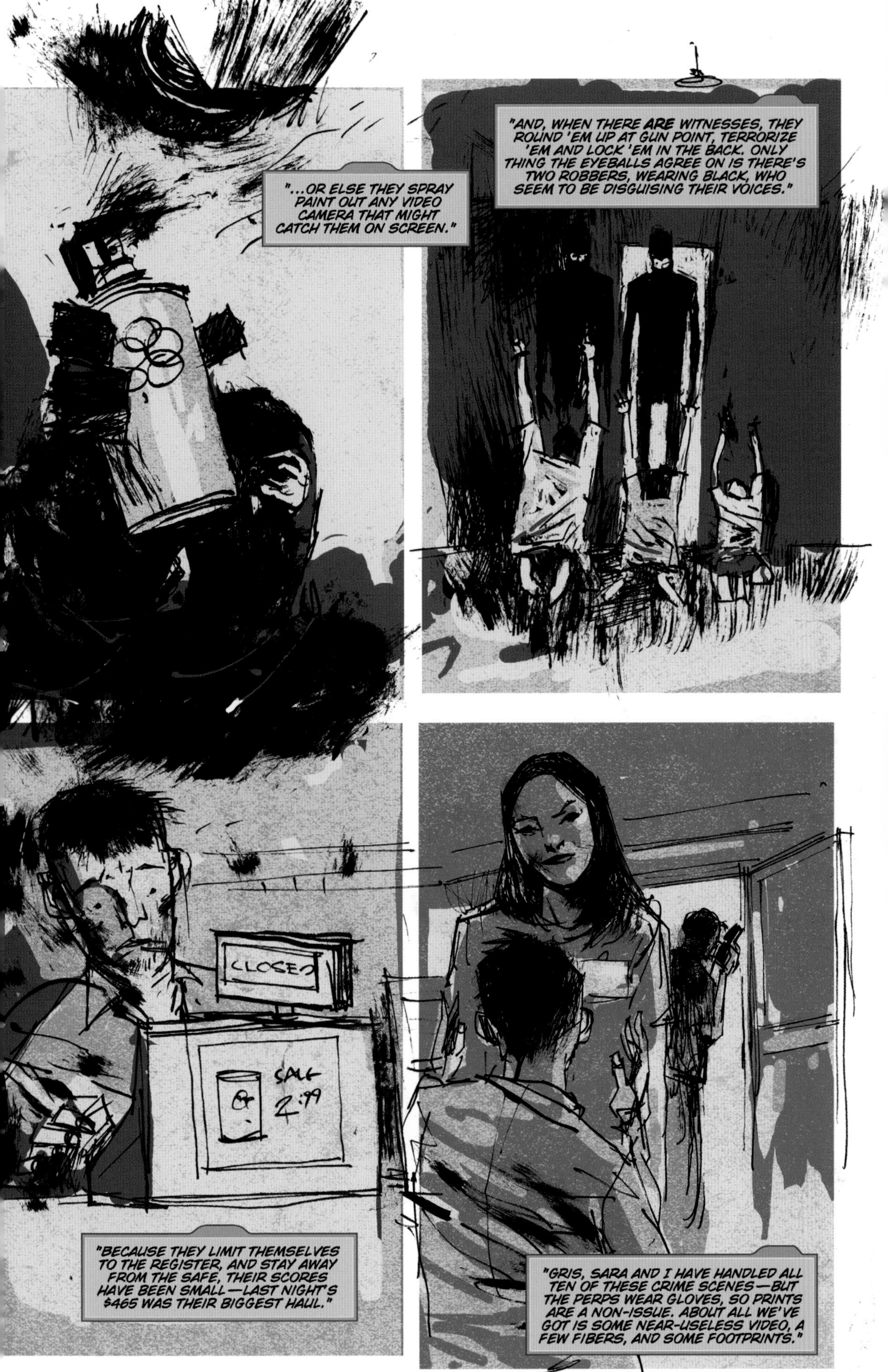
"...OR ELSE THEY SPRAY PAINT OUT ANY VIDEO CAMERA THAT MIGHT CATCH THEM ON SCREEN."
"AND, WHEN THERE ARE WITNESSES, THEY ROUND 'EM UP AT GUN POINT, TERRORIZE 'EM AND LOCK 'EM IN THE BACK. ONLY THING THE EYEBALLS AGREE ON IS THERE'S TWO ROBBERS, WEARING BLACK, WHO SEEM TO BE DISGUISING THEIR VOICES."
CLOSED
SALE 2.99
"BECAUSE THEY LIMIT THEMSELVES TO THE REGISTER, AND STAY AWAY FROM THE SAFE, THEIR SCORES HAVE BEEN SMALL—LAST NIGHT'S $465 WAS THEIR BIGGEST HAUL."
"GRIS, SARA AND I HAVE HANDLED ALL TEN OF THESE CRIME SCENES—BUT THE PERPS WEAR GLOVES, SO PRINTS ARE A NON-ISSUE. ABOUT ALL WE'VE GOT IS SOME NEAR-USELESS VIDEO, A FEW FIBERS, AND SOME FOOTPRINTS."

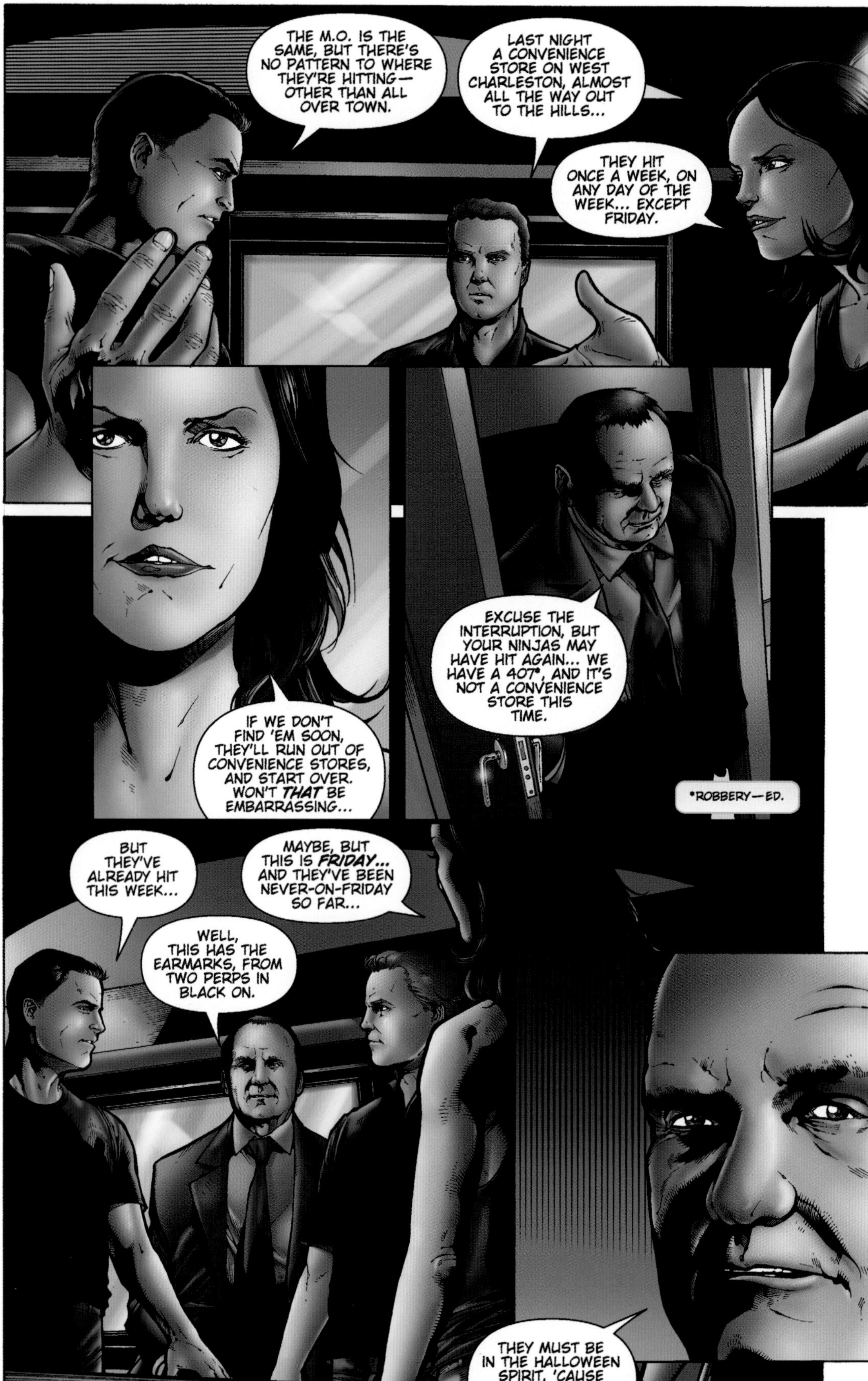
THE M.O. IS THE SAME, BUT THERE'S NO PATTERN TO WHERE THEY'RE HITTING—OTHER THAN ALL OVER TOWN.
LAST NIGHT A CONVENIENCE STORE ON WEST CHARLESTON, ALMOST ALL THE WAY OUT TO THE HILLS...
THEY HIT ONCE A WEEK, ON ANY DAY OF THE WEEK... EXCEPT FRIDAY.
IF WE DON'T FIND 'EM SOON, THEY'LL RUN OUT OF CONVENIENCE STORES, AND START OVER. WON'T THAT BE EMBARRASSING...
EXCUSE THE INTERRUPTION, BUT YOUR NINJAS MAY HAVE HIT AGAIN... WE HAVE A 407*, AND IT'S NOT A CONVENIENCE STORE THIS TIME.
*ROBBERY—ED.
BUT THEY'VE ALREADY HIT THIS WEEK...
MAYBE, BUT THIS IS FRIDAY... AND THEY'VE BEEN NEVER-ON-FRIDAY SO FAR...
WELL, THIS HAS THE EARMARKS, FROM TWO PERPS IN BLACK ON.
THEY MUST BE IN THE HALLOWEEN SPIRIT, 'CAUSE THEY'VE HIT A HAUNTED HOUSE...

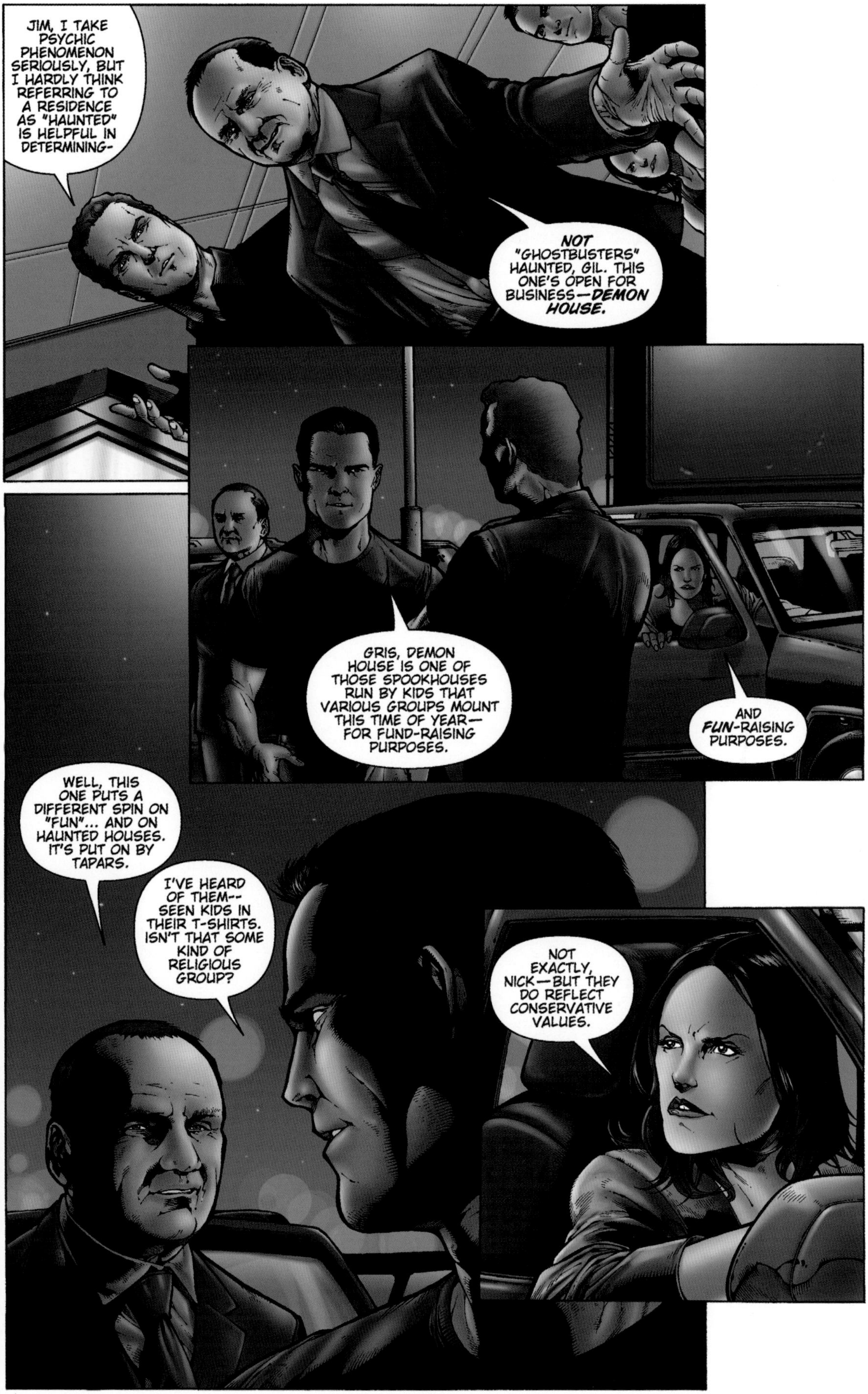
JIM, I TAKE PSYCHIC PHENOMENON SERIOUSLY, BUT I HARDLY THINK REFERRING TO A RESIDENCE AS "HAUNTED" IS HELPFUL IN DETERMINING-
NOT "GHOSTBUSTERS" HAUNTED, GIL. THIS ONE'S OPEN FOR BUSINESS—DEMON HOUSE.
GRIS, DEMON HOUSE IS ONE OF THOSE SPOOKHOUSES RUN BY KIDS THAT VARIOUS GROUPS MOUNT THIS TIME OF YEAR—FOR FUND-RAISING PURPOSES.
AND FUN-RAISING PURPOSES.
WELL, THIS ONE PUTS A DIFFERENT SPIN ON "FUN"... AND ON HAUNTED HOUSES. IT'S PUT ON BY TAPARS.
I'VE HEARD OF THEM-- SEEN KIDS IN THEIR T-SHIRTS. ISN'T THAT SOME KIND OF RELIGIOUS GROUP?
NOT EXACTLY, NICK—BUT THEY DO REFLECT CONSERVATIVE VALUES.

SO TAPARS IS AN ACRONYM FOR "TEENS AND PARENTS FOR A RESPONSIBLE SOCIETY"? THAT DOESN'T EXACTLY SOUND LIKE THE KIND OF GOOD TIME MOST KIDS ARE LOOKING FOR...

YOU'D BE SURPRISED, NICK.

I SAW A TV NEWS STORY ON DEMON HOUSE LAST YEAR. THEY PUT ON AN ELABORATE SHOW, A WHOLE SERIES OF HORRIFIC SCENES...

YES, AND MY UNDERSTANDING IS THE KIDS INVOLVED HAVE A GREAT TIME DOING THE PLAY-ACTING...

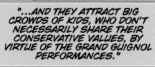

"...AND THEY ATTRACT BIG CROWDS OF KIDS, WHO DON'T NECESSARILY SHARE THEIR CONSERVATIVE VALUES, BY VIRTUE OF THE GRAND GUIGNOL PERFORMANCES."

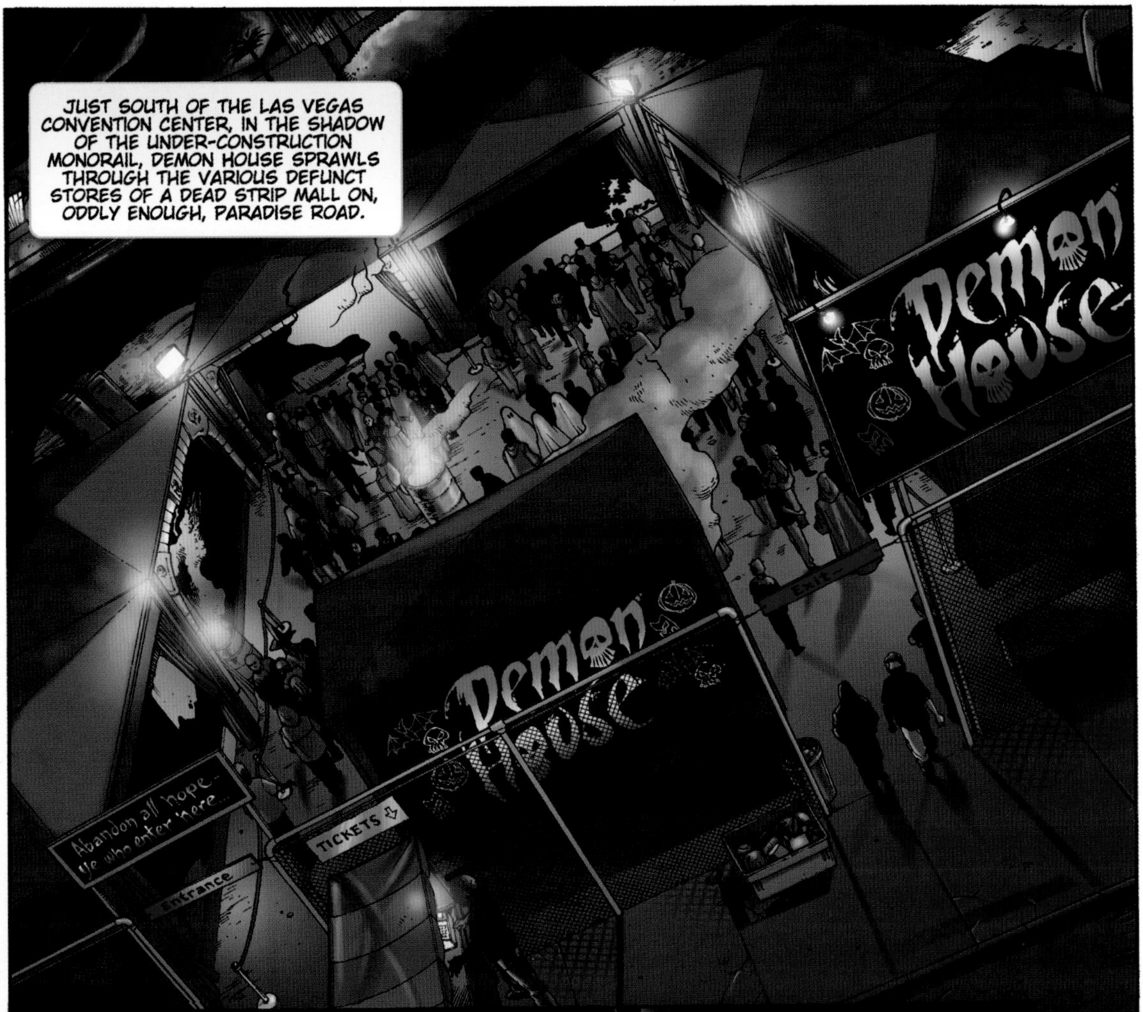
JUST SOUTH OF THE LAS VEGAS CONVENTION CENTER, IN THE SHADOW OF THE UNDER-CONSTRUCTION MONORAIL, DEMON HOUSE SPRAWLS THROUGH THE VARIOUS DEFUNCT STORES OF A DEAD STRIP MALL ON, ODDLY ENOUGH, PARADISE ROAD.
Demon House
Demon House
Abandon all hope- ye who enter here...
TICKETS
Entrance
Exit

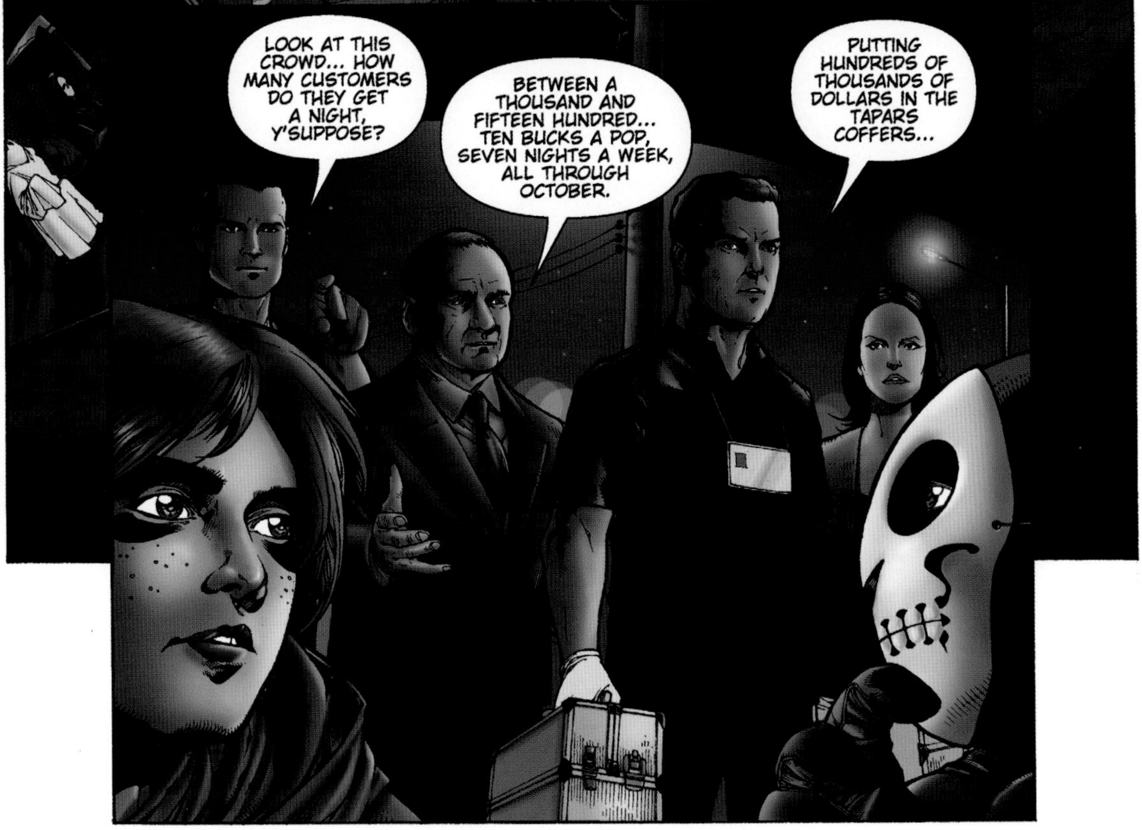
LOOK AT THIS CROWD... HOW MANY CUSTOMERS DO THEY GET A NIGHT, Y'SUPPOSE?
BETWEEN A THOUSAND AND FIFTEEN HUNDRED... TEN BUCKS A POP, SEVEN NIGHTS A WEEK, ALL THROUGH OCTOBER.
PUTTING HUNDREDS OF THOUSANDS OF DOLLARS IN THE TAPARS COFFERS...

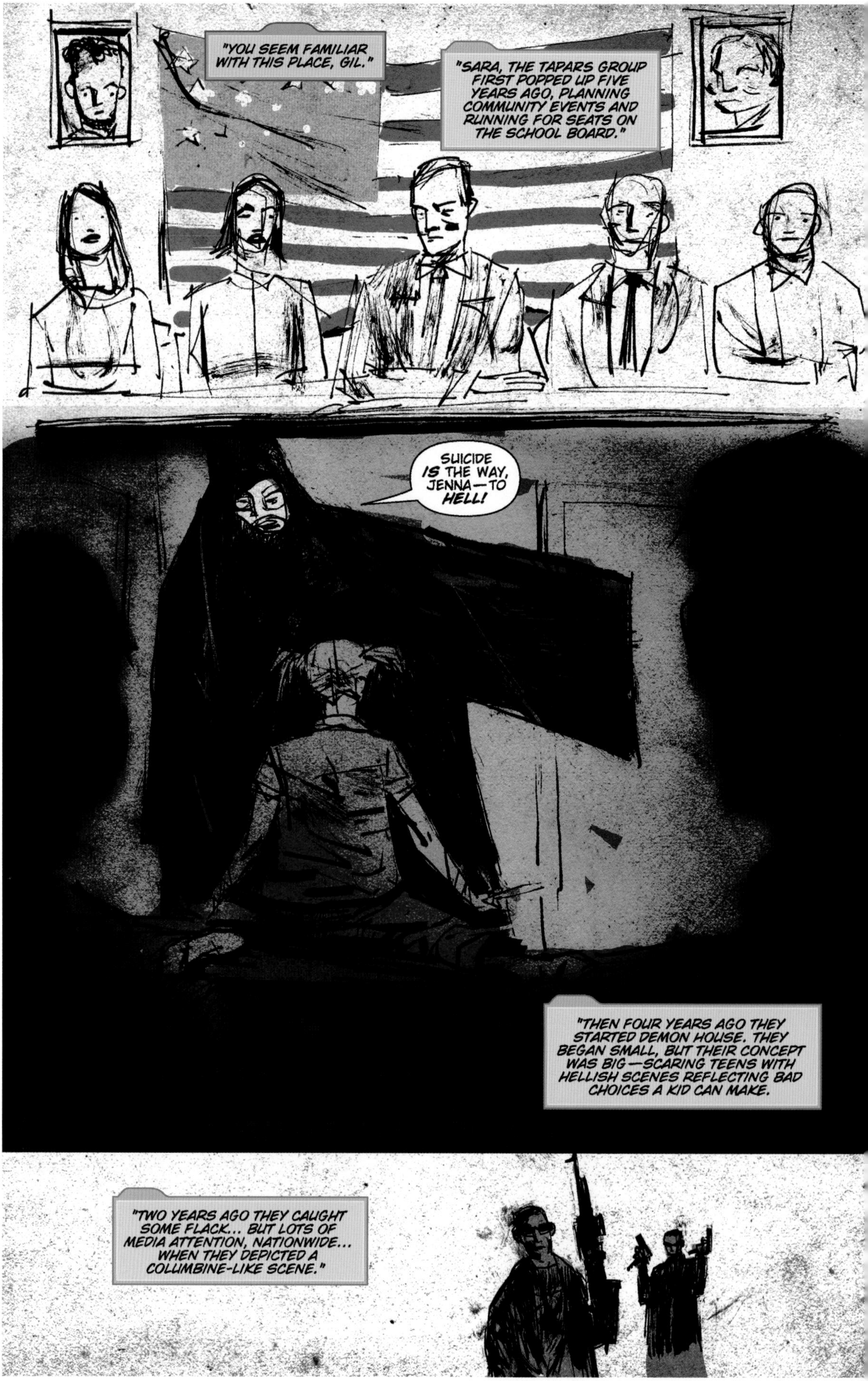
"YOU SEEM FAMILIAR WITH THIS PLACE, GIL."
"SARA, THE TAPARS GROUP FIRST POPPED UP FIVE YEARS AGO, PLANNING COMMUNITY EVENTS AND RUNNING FOR SEATS ON THE SCHOOL BOARD."
SUICIDE *IS* THE WAY, JENNA—TO *HELL!*
"THEN FOUR YEARS AGO THEY STARTED DEMON HOUSE. THEY BEGAN SMALL, BUT THEIR CONCEPT WAS BIG—SCARING TEENS WITH HELLISH SCENES REFLECTING BAD CHOICES A KID CAN MAKE.
"TWO YEARS AGO THEY CAUGHT SOME FLACK... BUT LOTS OF MEDIA ATTENTION, NATIONWIDE... WHEN THEY DEPICTED A COLUMBINE-LIKE SCENE."

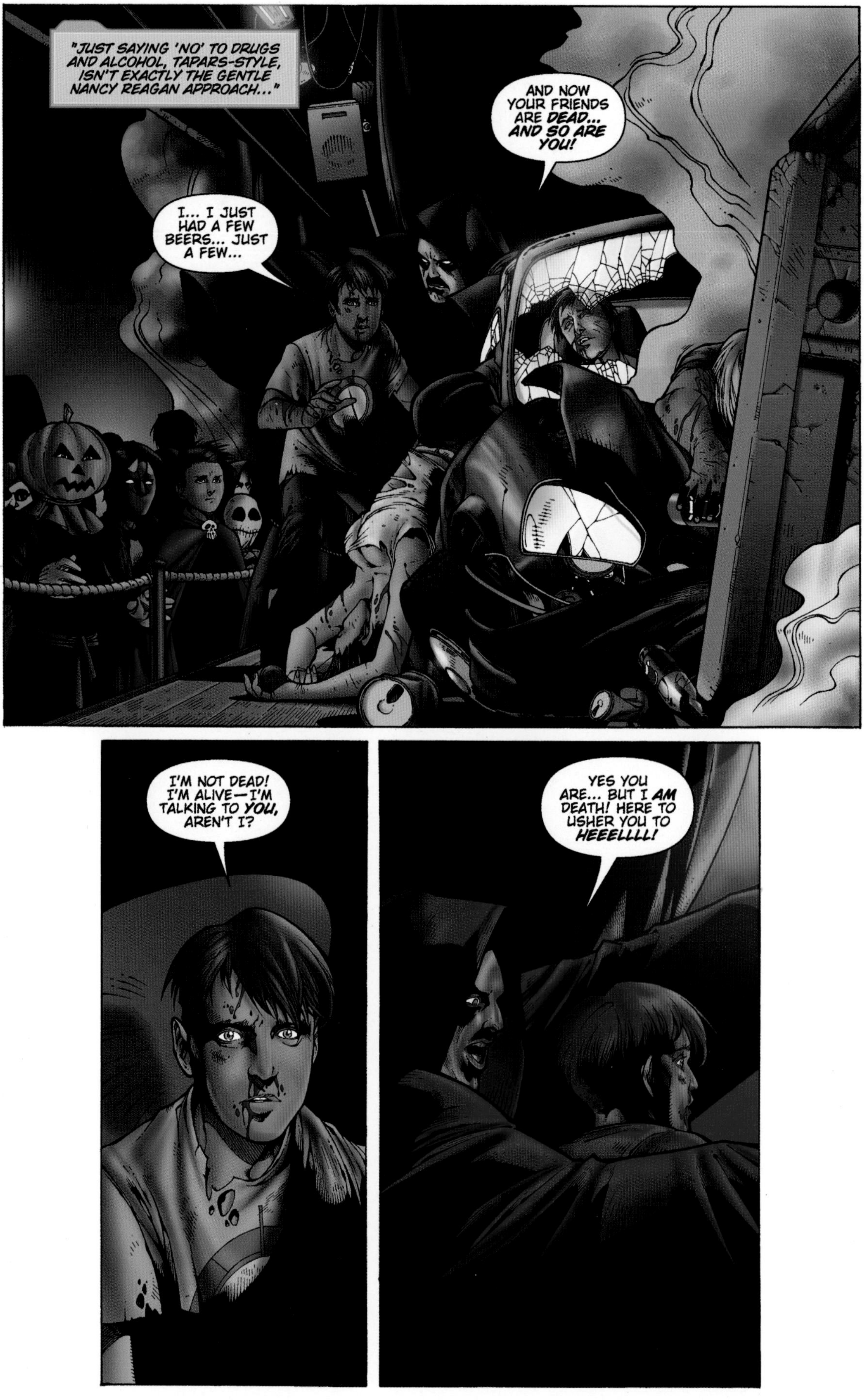
"JUST SAYING 'NO' TO DRUGS AND ALCOHOL, TAPARS-STYLE, ISN'T EXACTLY THE GENTLE NANCY REAGAN APPROACH..."
AND NOW YOUR FRIENDS ARE DEAD... AND SO ARE YOU!
I... I JUST HAD A FEW BEERS... JUST A FEW...
I'M NOT DEAD! I'M ALIVE—I'M TALKING TO YOU, AREN'T I?
YES YOU ARE... BUT I AM DEATH! HERE TO USHER YOU TO HEEELLLL!

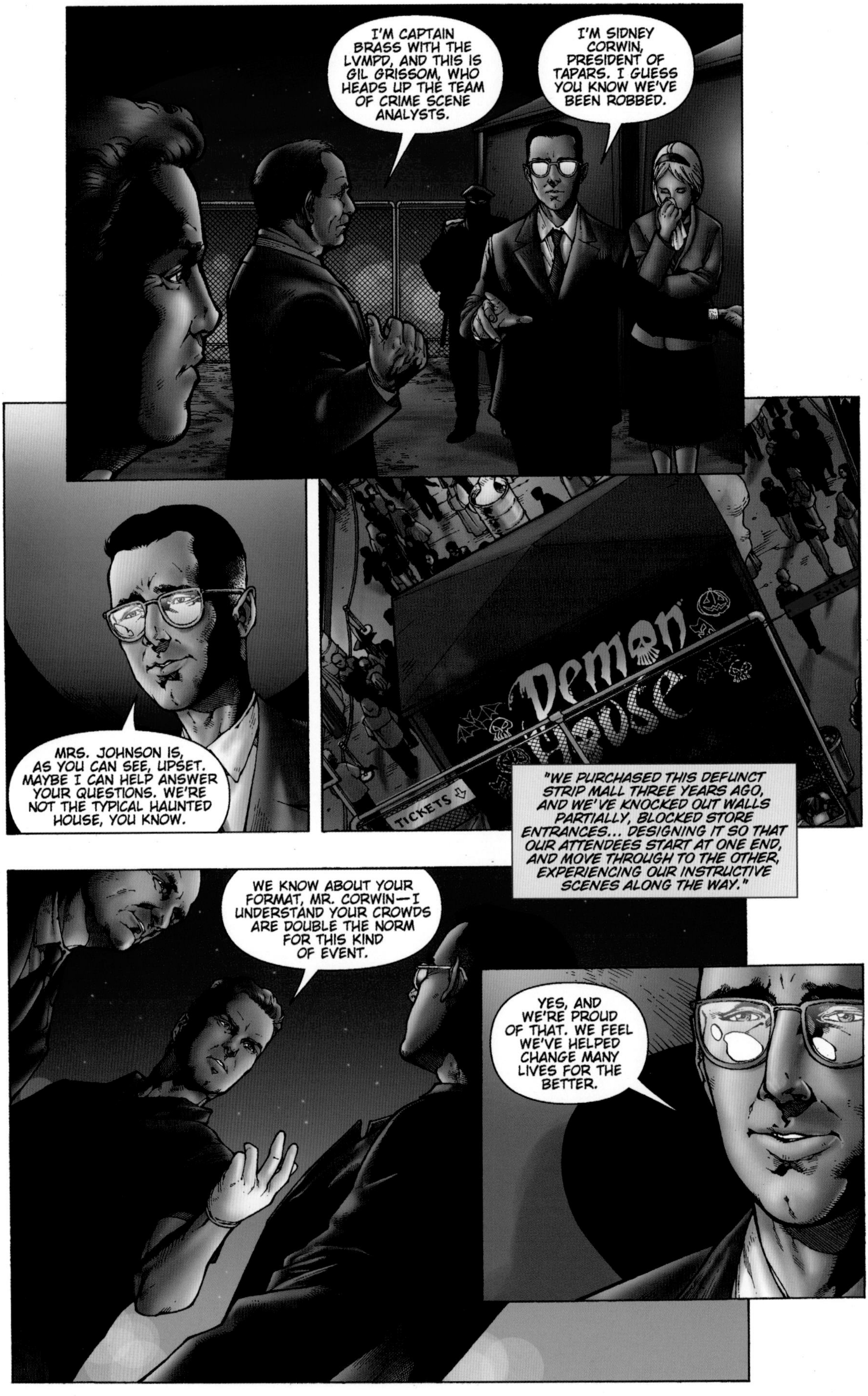
I'M CAPTAIN BRASS WITH THE LVMPD, AND THIS IS GIL GRISSOM, WHO HEADS UP THE TEAM OF CRIME SCENE ANALYSTS.
I'M SIDNEY CORWIN, PRESIDENT OF TAPARS. I GUESS YOU KNOW WE'VE BEEN ROBBED.
MRS. JOHNSON IS, AS YOU CAN SEE, UPSET. MAYBE I CAN HELP ANSWER YOUR QUESTIONS. WE'RE NOT THE TYPICAL HAUNTED HOUSE, YOU KNOW.
Demon House
TICKETS
Exit
"WE PURCHASED THIS DEFUNCT STRIP MALL THREE YEARS AGO, AND WE'VE KNOCKED OUT WALLS PARTIALLY, BLOCKED STORE ENTRANCES... DESIGNING IT SO THAT OUR ATTENDEES START AT ONE END, AND MOVE THROUGH TO THE OTHER, EXPERIENCING OUR INSTRUCTIVE SCENES ALONG THE WAY."
WE KNOW ABOUT YOUR FORMAT, MR. CORWIN—I UNDERSTAND YOUR CROWDS ARE DOUBLE THE NORM FOR THIS KIND OF EVENT.
YES, AND WE'RE PROUD OF THAT. WE FEEL WE'VE HELPED CHANGE MANY LIVES FOR THE BETTER.

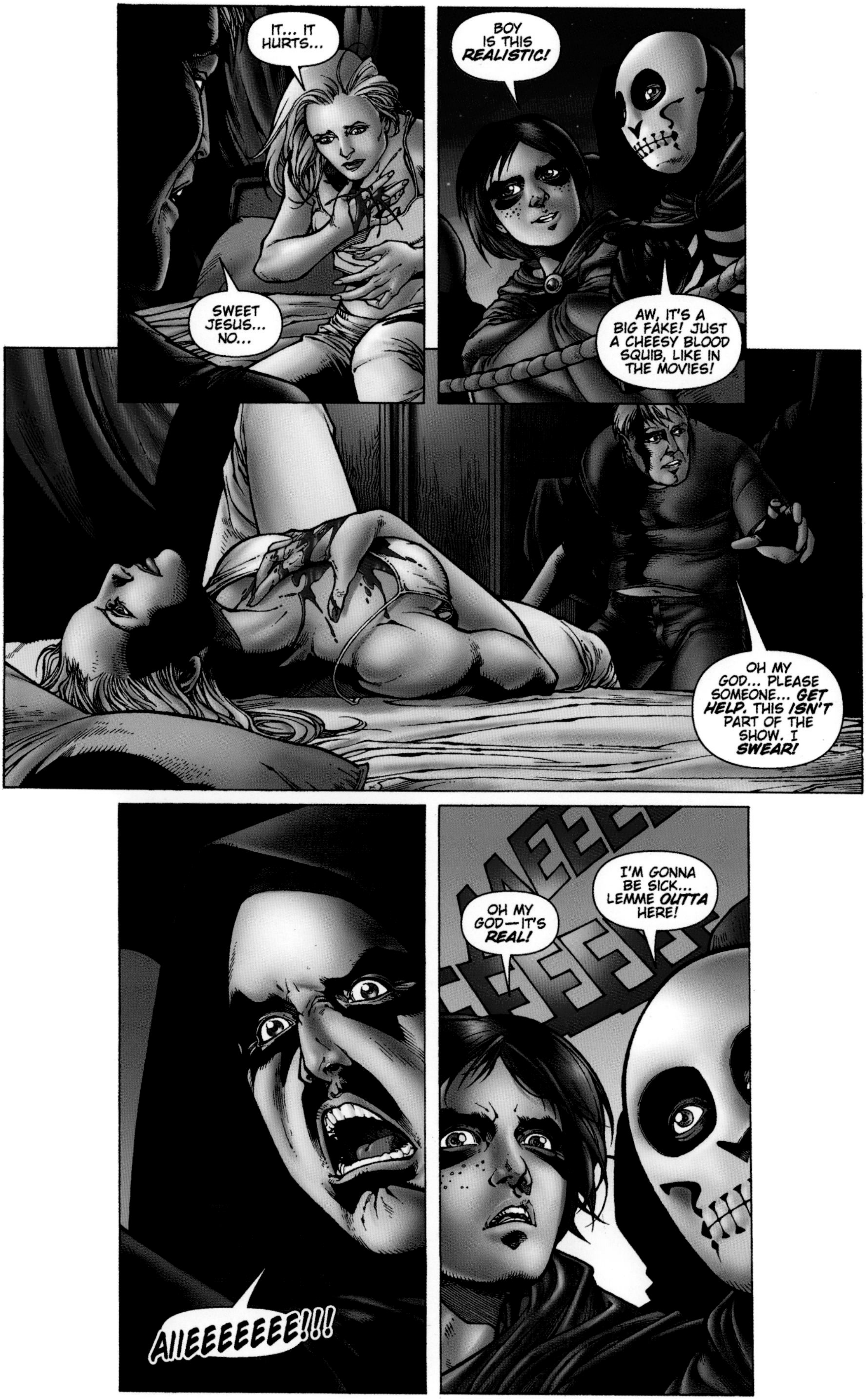
IT... IT HURTS...
SWEET JESUS... NO...
BOY IS THIS *REALISTIC!*
AW, IT'S A BIG FAKE! JUST A CHEESY BLOOD SQUIB, LIKE IN THE MOVIES!
OH MY GOD... PLEASE SOMEONE... **GET HELP.** THIS **ISN'T** PART OF THE SHOW. I **SWEAR!**
AIIEEEEEEEE!!!
OH MY GOD—IT'S *REAL!*
I'M GONNA BE SICK... LEMME *OUTTA* HERE!

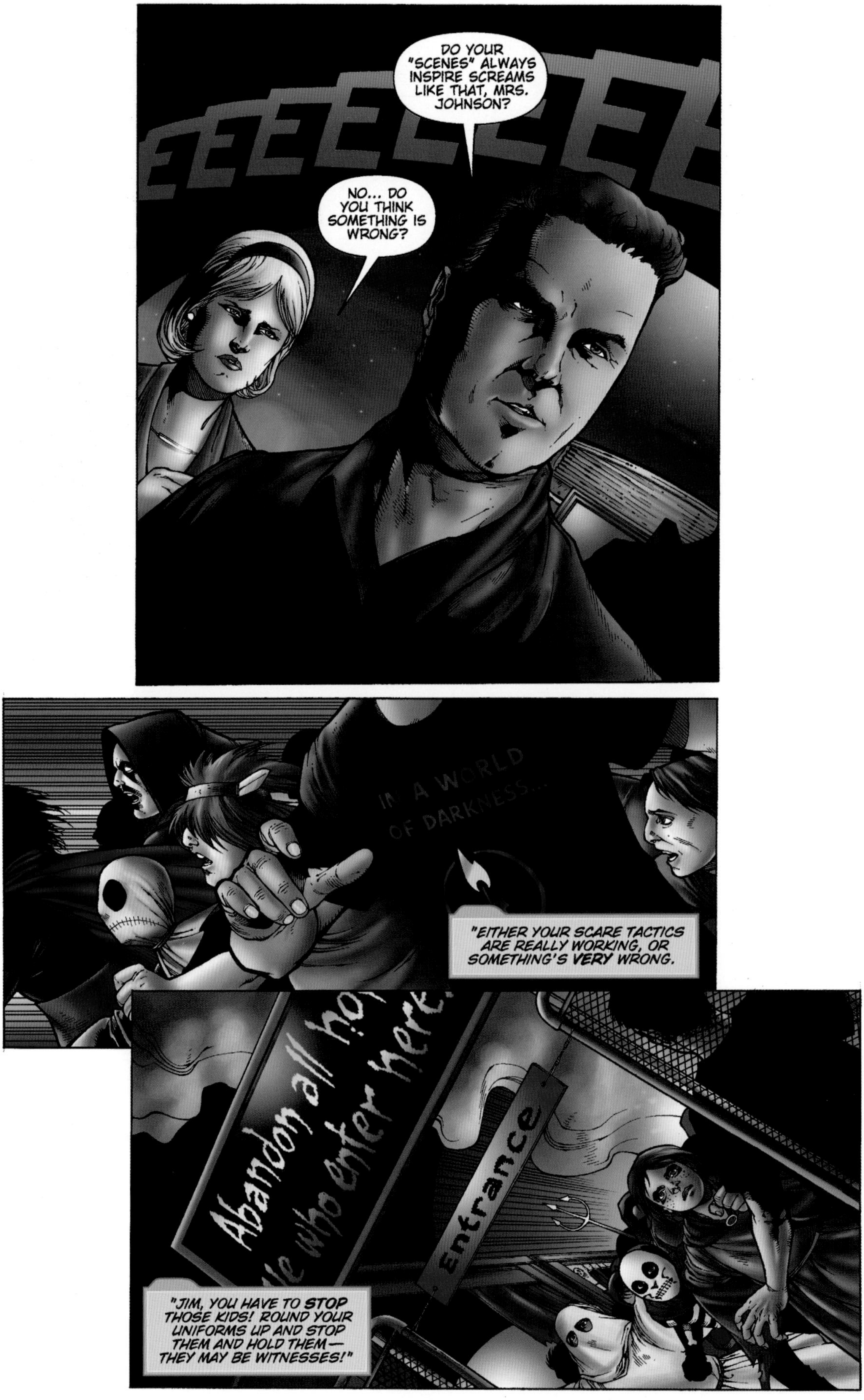
DO YOUR "SCENES" ALWAYS INSPIRE SCREAMS LIKE THAT, MRS. JOHNSON?
NO... DO YOU THINK SOMETHING IS WRONG?
"EITHER YOUR SCARE TACTICS ARE REALLY WORKING, OR SOMETHING'S **VERY** WRONG.
Entrance
"JIM, YOU HAVE TO **STOP** THOSE KIDS! ROUND YOUR UNIFORMS UP AND STOP THEM AND HOLD THEM— THEY MAY BE WITNESSES!"

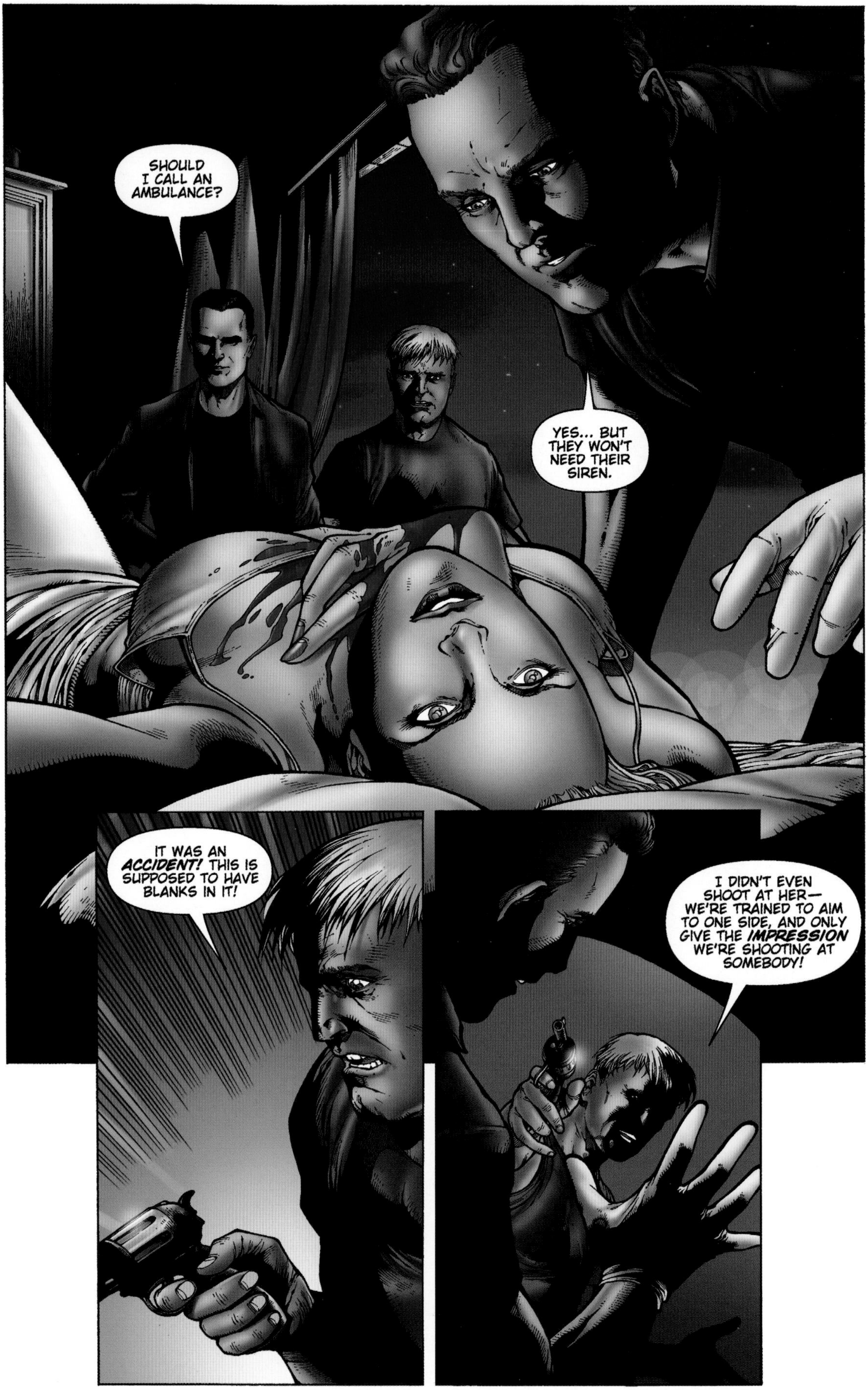
SHOULD I CALL AN AMBULANCE?
YES... BUT THEY WON'T NEED THEIR SIREN.
IT WAS AN *ACCIDENT!* THIS IS SUPPOSED TO HAVE BLANKS IN IT!
I DIDN'T EVEN SHOOT AT HER— WE'RE TRAINED TO AIM TO ONE SIDE, AND ONLY GIVE THE *IMPRESSION* WE'RE SHOOTING AT SOMEBODY!

Chapter 2
"Magic Town"

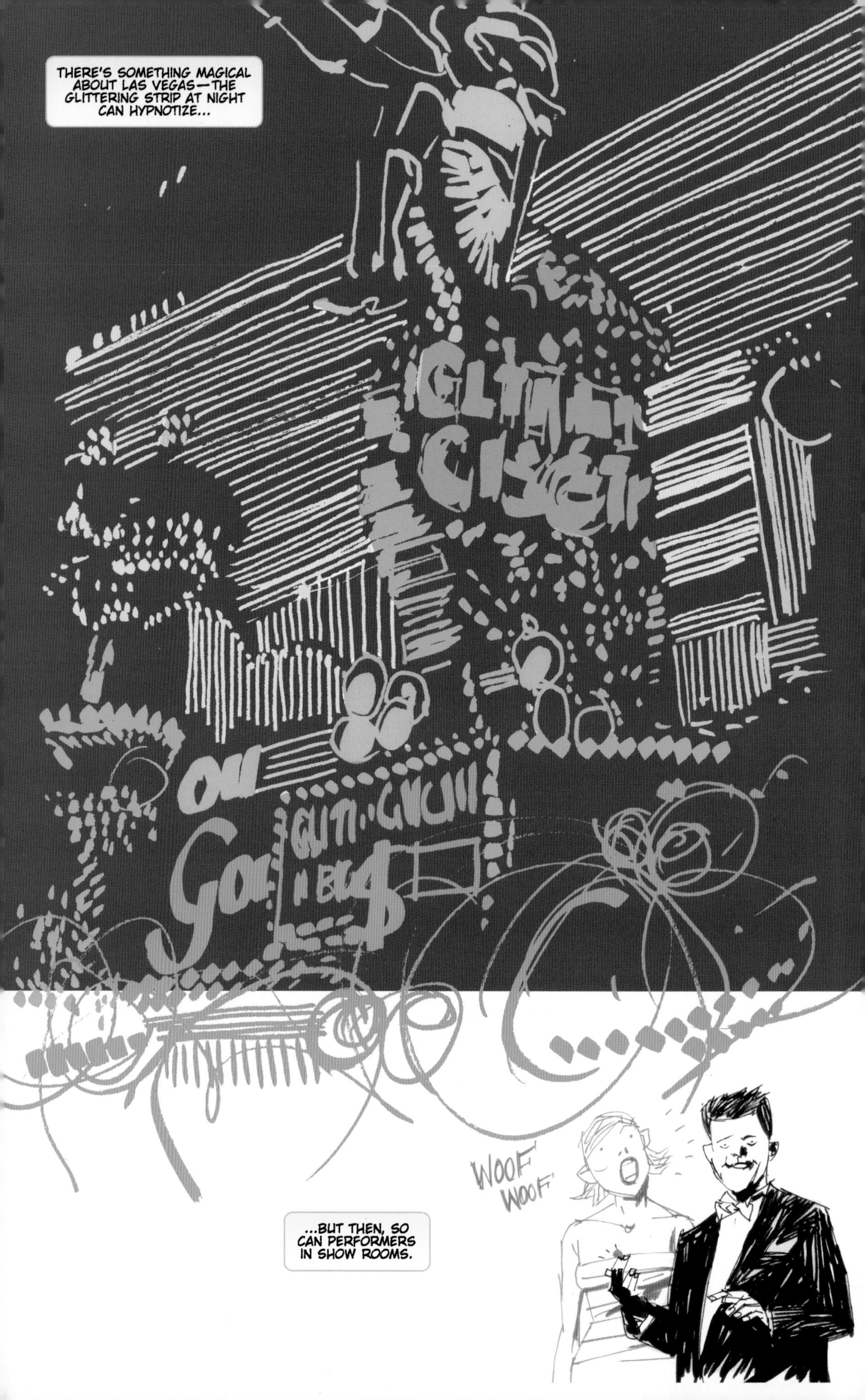
THERE'S SOMETHING MAGICAL ABOUT LAS VEGAS—THE GLITTERING STRIP AT NIGHT CAN HYPNOTIZE...
WOOF WOOF
...BUT THEN, SO CAN PERFORMERS IN SHOW ROOMS.

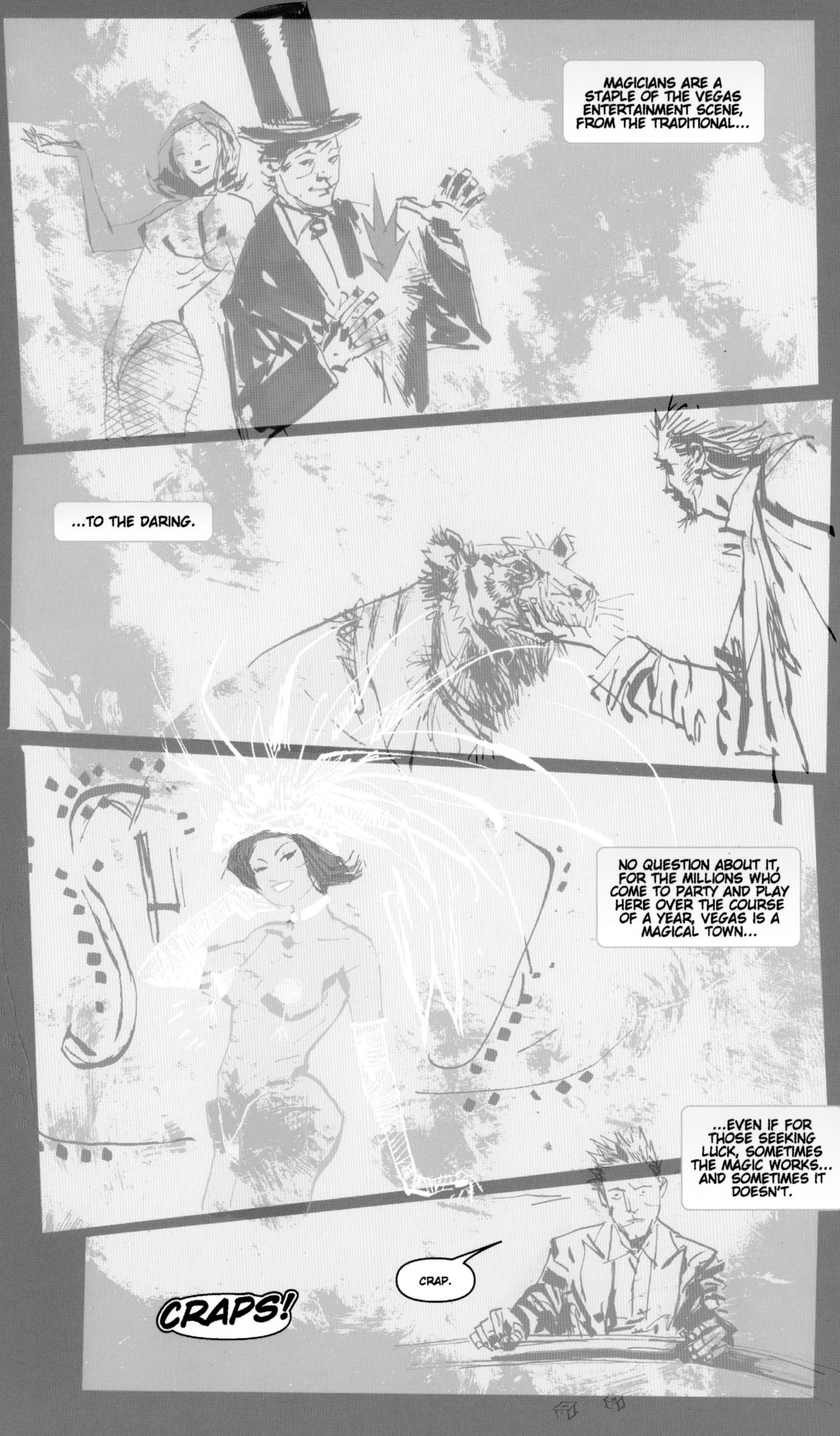
MAGICIANS ARE A STAPLE OF THE VEGAS ENTERTAINMENT SCENE, FROM THE TRADITIONAL...
...TO THE DARING.
NO QUESTION ABOUT IT, FOR THE MILLIONS WHO COME TO PARTY AND PLAY HERE OVER THE COURSE OF A YEAR, VEGAS IS A MAGICAL TOWN...
...EVEN IF FOR THOSE SEEKING LUCK, SOMETIMES THE MAGIC WORKS... AND SOMETIMES IT DOESN'T.
CRAPS!
CRAP.

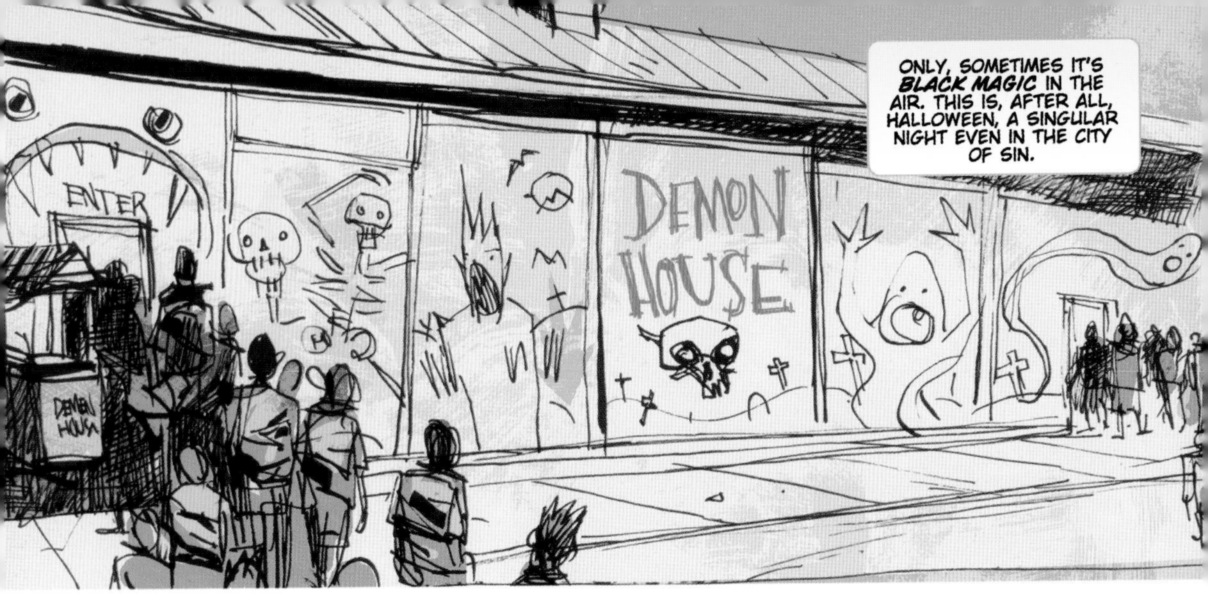
ONLY, SOMETIMES IT'S ***BLACK MAGIC*** IN THE AIR. THIS IS, AFTER ALL, HALLOWEEN, A SINGULAR NIGHT EVEN IN THE CITY OF SIN.
ENTER
DEMON HOUSE
DEMON HOUSE

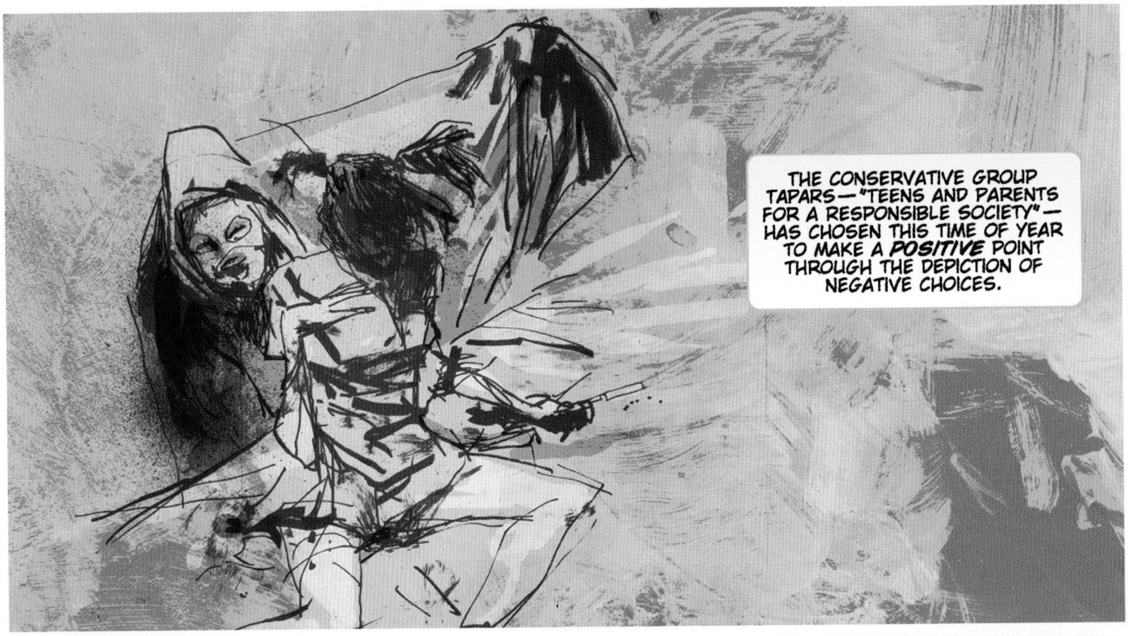
THE CONSERVATIVE GROUP TAPARS—"TEENS AND PARENTS FOR A RESPONSIBLE SOCIETY"—HAS CHOSEN THIS TIME OF YEAR TO MAKE A ***POSITIVE*** POINT THROUGH THE DEPICTION OF NEGATIVE CHOICES.

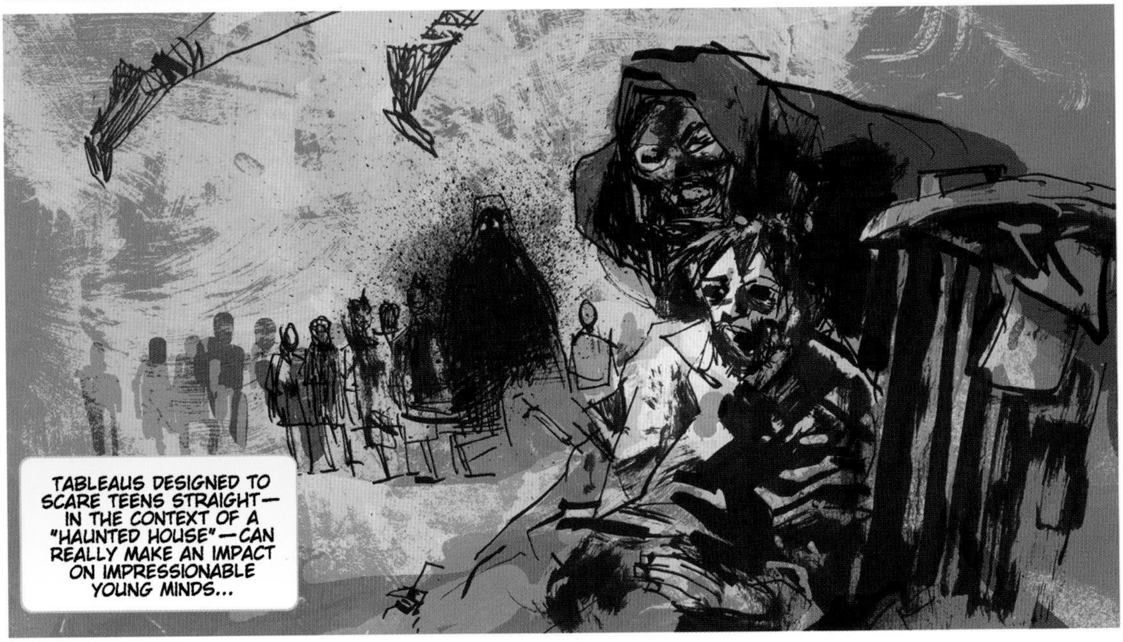
TABLEAUS DESIGNED TO SCARE TEENS STRAIGHT—IN THE CONTEXT OF A "HAUNTED HOUSE"—CAN REALLY MAKE AN IMPACT ON IMPRESSIONABLE YOUNG MINDS...

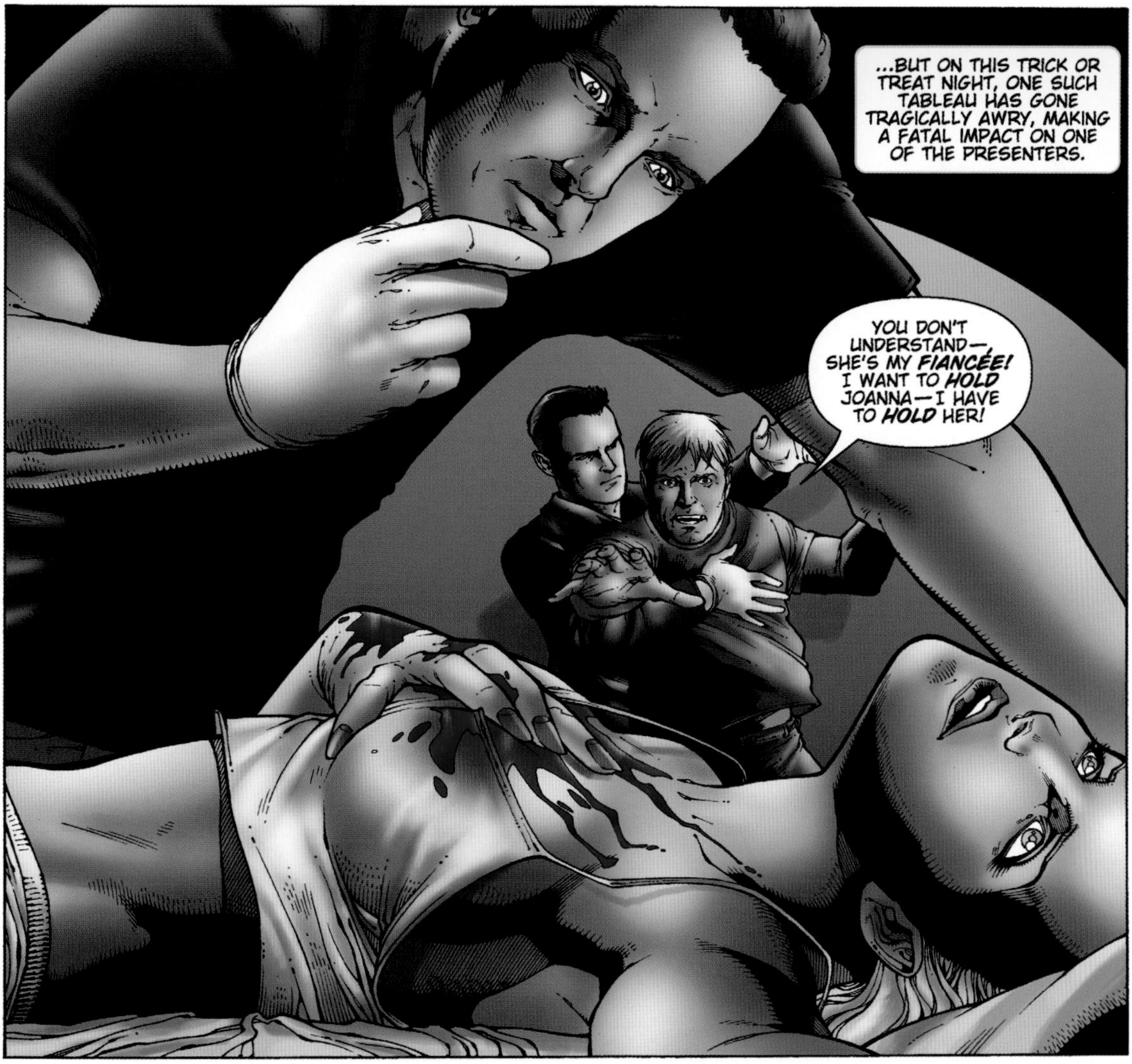
...BUT ON THIS TRICK OR TREAT NIGHT, ONE SUCH TABLEAU HAS GONE TRAGICALLY AWRY, MAKING A FATAL IMPACT ON ONE OF THE PRESENTERS.
YOU DON'T UNDERSTAND—SHE'S MY FIANCÉE! I WANT TO HOLD JOANNA—I HAVE TO HOLD HER!

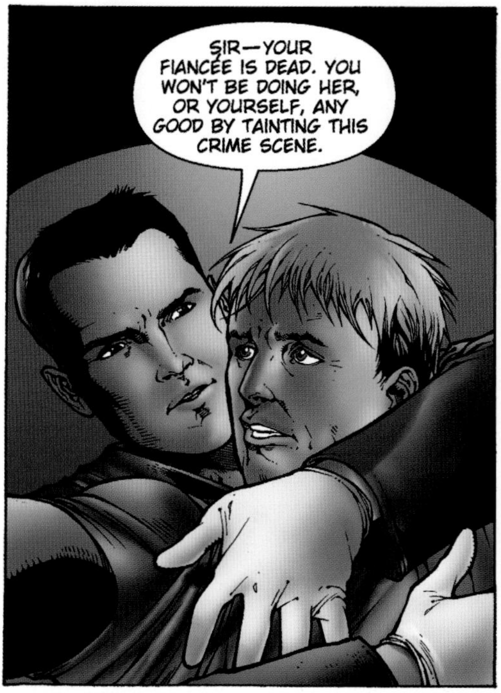
SIR—YOUR FIANCÉE IS DEAD. YOU WON'T BE DOING HER, OR YOURSELF, ANY GOOD BY TAINTING THIS CRIME SCENE.

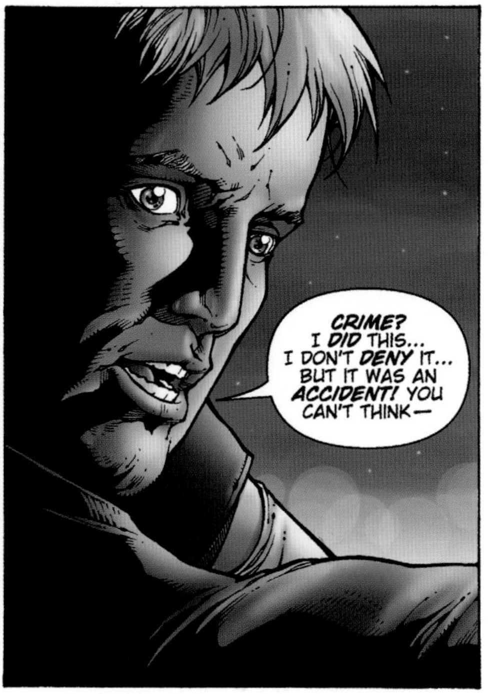
CRIME? I DID THIS... I DON'T DENY IT... BUT IT WAS AN ACCIDENT! YOU CAN'T THINK—

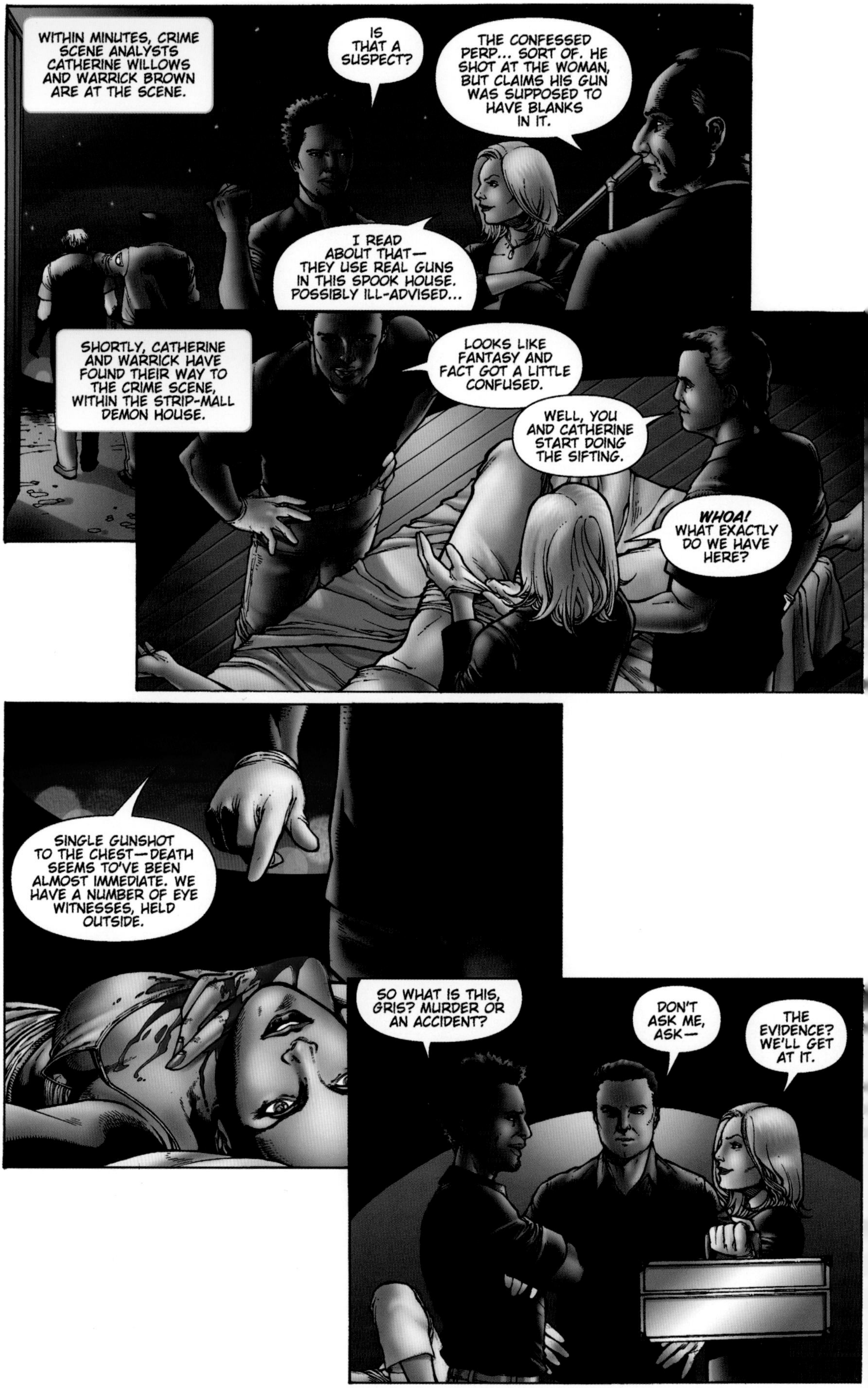
WITHIN MINUTES, CRIME SCENE ANALYSTS CATHERINE WILLOWS AND WARRICK BROWN ARE AT THE SCENE.
IS THAT A SUSPECT?
THE CONFESSED PERP... SORT OF. HE SHOT AT THE WOMAN, BUT CLAIMS HIS GUN WAS SUPPOSED TO HAVE BLANKS IN IT.
I READ ABOUT THAT— THEY USE REAL GUNS IN THIS SPOOK HOUSE. POSSIBLY ILL-ADVISED...
SHORTLY, CATHERINE AND WARRICK HAVE FOUND THEIR WAY TO THE CRIME SCENE, WITHIN THE STRIP-MALL DEMON HOUSE.
LOOKS LIKE FANTASY AND FACT GOT A LITTLE CONFUSED.
WELL, YOU AND CATHERINE START DOING THE SIFTING.
WHOA! WHAT EXACTLY DO WE HAVE HERE?
SINGLE GUNSHOT TO THE CHEST—DEATH SEEMS TO'VE BEEN ALMOST IMMEDIATE. WE HAVE A NUMBER OF EYE WITNESSES, HELD OUTSIDE.
SO WHAT IS THIS, GRIS? MURDER OR AN ACCIDENT?
DON'T ASK ME, ASK—
THE EVIDENCE? WE'LL GET AT IT.

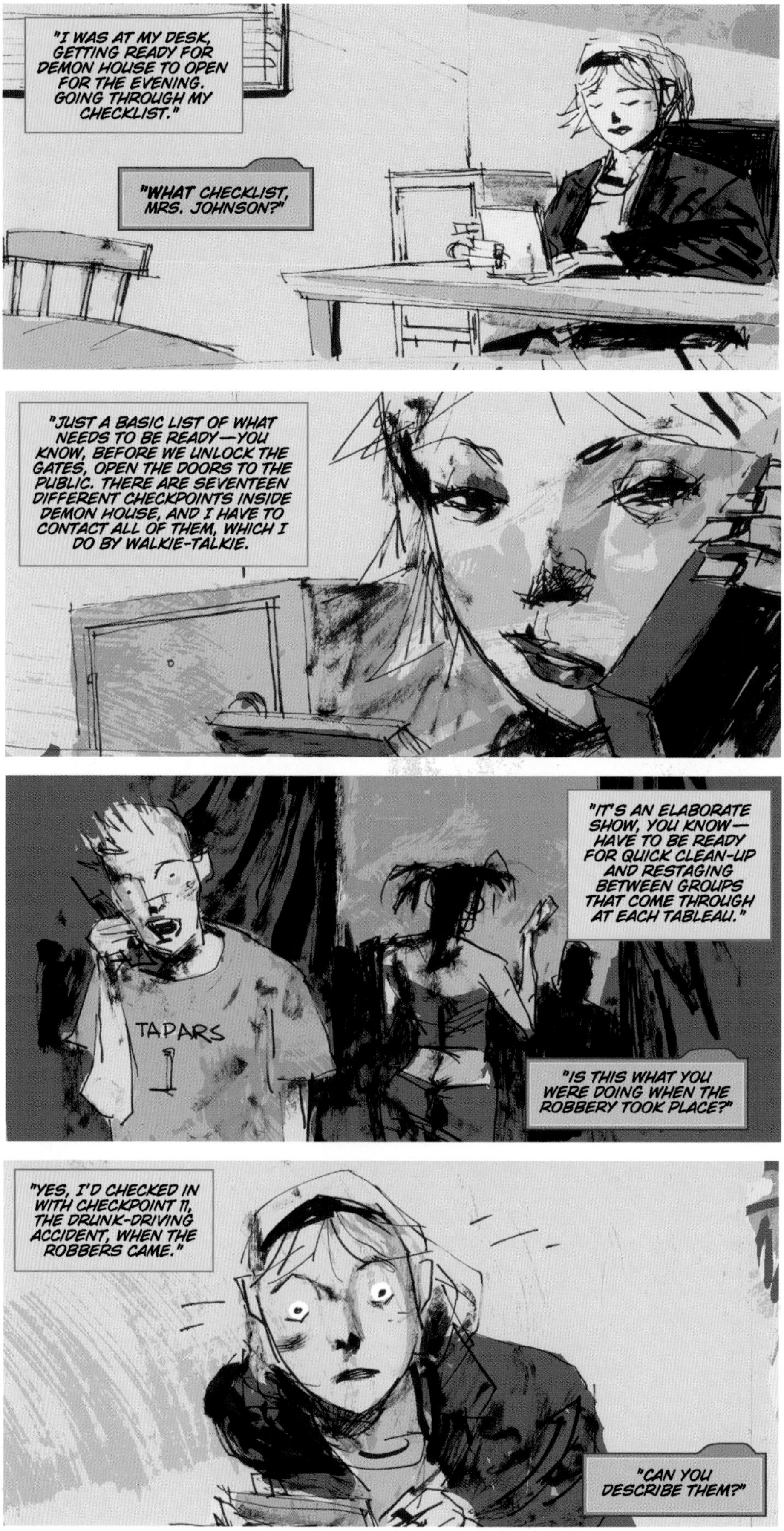
"I WAS AT MY DESK, GETTING READY FOR DEMON HOUSE TO OPEN FOR THE EVENING. GOING THROUGH MY CHECKLIST."
"WHAT CHECKLIST, MRS. JOHNSON?"
"JUST A BASIC LIST OF WHAT NEEDS TO BE READY—YOU KNOW, BEFORE WE UNLOCK THE GATES, OPEN THE DOORS TO THE PUBLIC. THERE ARE SEVENTEEN DIFFERENT CHECKPOINTS INSIDE DEMON HOUSE, AND I HAVE TO CONTACT ALL OF THEM, WHICH I DO BY WALKIE-TALKIE.
"IT'S AN ELABORATE SHOW, YOU KNOW—HAVE TO BE READY FOR QUICK CLEAN-UP AND RESTAGING BETWEEN GROUPS THAT COME THROUGH AT EACH TABLEAU."
TAPARS
"IS THIS WHAT YOU WERE DOING WHEN THE ROBBERY TOOK PLACE?"
"YES, I'D CHECKED IN WITH CHECKPOINT 11, THE DRUNK-DRIVING ACCIDENT, WHEN THE ROBBERS CAME."
"CAN YOU DESCRIBE THEM?"

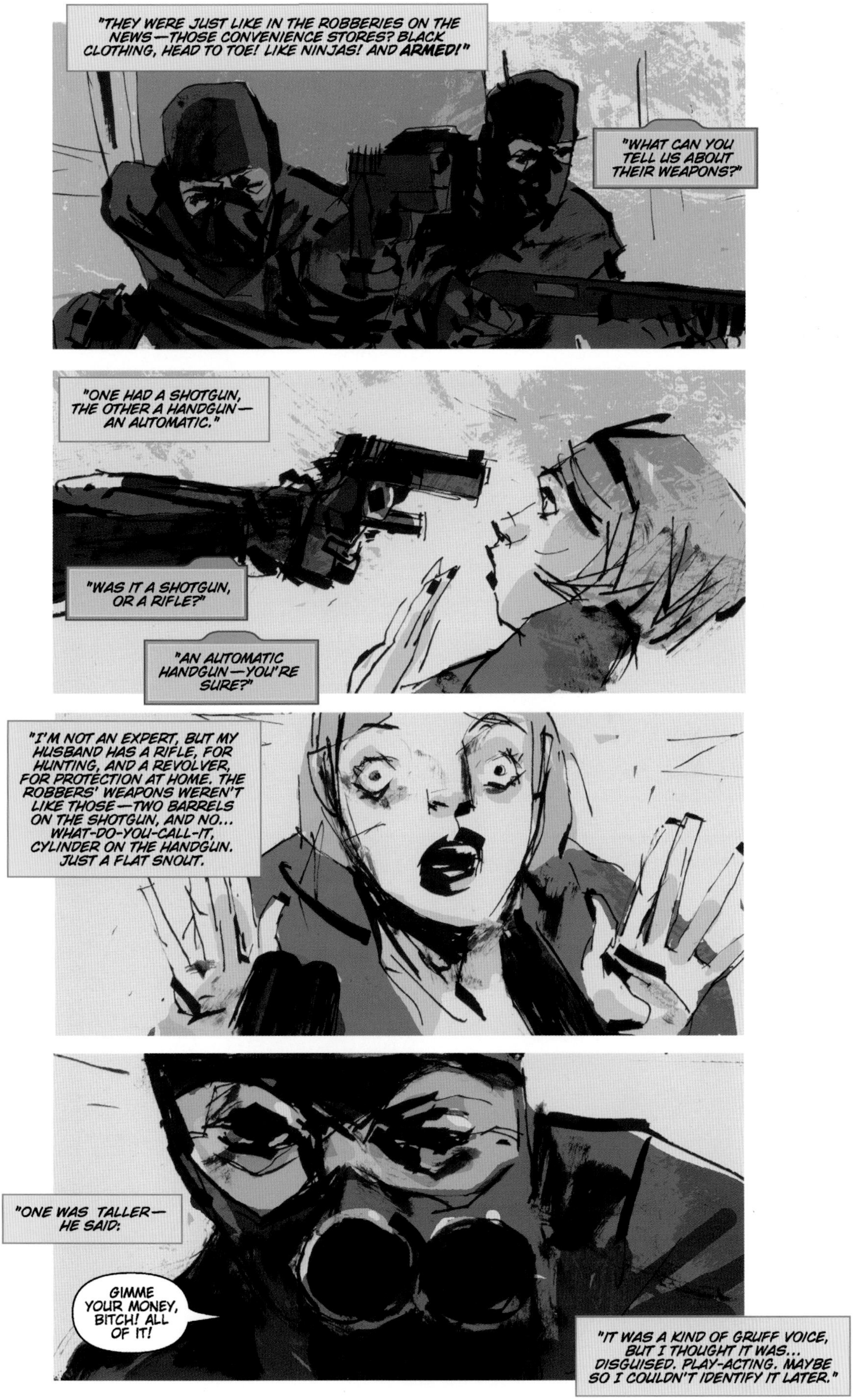
"THEY WERE JUST LIKE IN THE ROBBERIES ON THE NEWS—THOSE CONVENIENCE STORES? BLACK CLOTHING, HEAD TO TOE! LIKE NINJAS! AND ARMED!"
"WHAT CAN YOU TELL US ABOUT THEIR WEAPONS?"
"ONE HAD A SHOTGUN, THE OTHER A HANDGUN—AN AUTOMATIC."
"WAS IT A SHOTGUN, OR A RIFLE?"
"AN AUTOMATIC HANDGUN—YOU'RE SURE?"
"I'M NOT AN EXPERT, BUT MY HUSBAND HAS A RIFLE, FOR HUNTING, AND A REVOLVER, FOR PROTECTION AT HOME. THE ROBBERS' WEAPONS WEREN'T LIKE THOSE—TWO BARRELS ON THE SHOTGUN, AND NO... WHAT-DO-YOU-CALL-IT, CYLINDER ON THE HANDGUN. JUST A FLAT SNOUT.
"ONE WAS TALLER—HE SAID:
GIMME YOUR MONEY, BITCH! ALL OF IT!
"IT WAS A KIND OF GRUFF VOICE, BUT I THOUGHT IT WAS... DISGUISED. PLAY-ACTING. MAYBE SO I COULDN'T IDENTIFY IT LATER."

ANYWAY, I GAVE THEM THE PETTY CASH—THERE'S ALWAYS PETTY CASH IN MY DESK.

EVERYBODY— PRETTY MUCH COMMON KNOWLEDGE. THESE WERE SMALLER BILLS, ONES FOR MATERIALS AND WHAT-NOT. SPUR-OF-THE-MOMENT STUFF GETS PAID OUT OF THERE, Y'KNOW.

WHO WOULD KNOW THAT?

HOW MUCH?

MAYBE... THREE HUNDRED DOLLARS? BUT THAT'S WHEN THEY TOLD ME THEY WANTED THE MONEY FROM THE SAFE.

AND WHO KNEW ABOUT THAT?

"THE TAPARS COUNCIL—EIGHT OF US, IN ADDITION TO OUR PRESIDENT, SIDNEY CORWIN—YOU MET SIDNEY EARLIER."

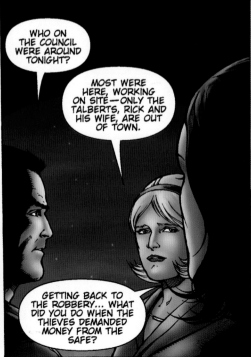

WHO ON THE COUNCIL WERE AROUND TONIGHT?

MOST WERE HERE, WORKING ON SITE—ONLY THE TALBERTS, RICK AND HIS WIFE, ARE OUT OF TOWN.

GETTING BACK TO THE ROBBERY... WHAT DID YOU DO WHEN THE THIEVES DEMANDED MONEY FROM THE SAFE?

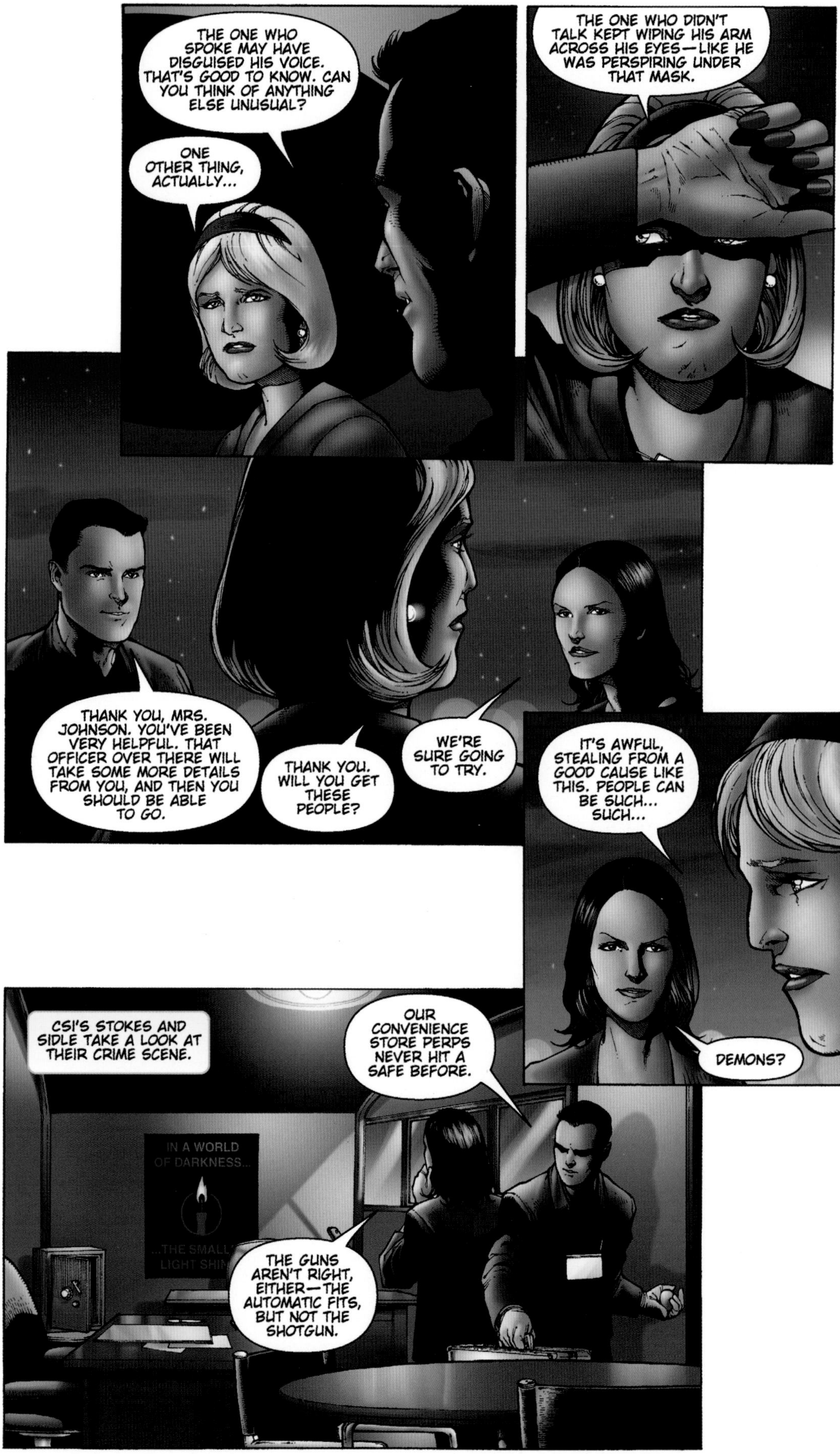
THE ONE WHO SPOKE MAY HAVE DISGUISED HIS VOICE. THAT'S GOOD TO KNOW. CAN YOU THINK OF ANYTHING ELSE UNUSUAL?
ONE OTHER THING, ACTUALLY...
THE ONE WHO DIDN'T TALK KEPT WIPING HIS ARM ACROSS HIS EYES—LIKE HE WAS PERSPIRING UNDER THAT MASK.
THANK YOU, MRS. JOHNSON. YOU'VE BEEN VERY HELPFUL. THAT OFFICER OVER THERE WILL TAKE SOME MORE DETAILS FROM YOU, AND THEN YOU SHOULD BE ABLE TO GO.
THANK YOU. WILL YOU GET THESE PEOPLE?
WE'RE SURE GOING TO TRY.
IT'S AWFUL, STEALING FROM A GOOD CAUSE LIKE THIS. PEOPLE CAN BE SUCH... SUCH...
DEMONS?
CSI'S STOKES AND SIDLE TAKE A LOOK AT THEIR CRIME SCENE.
OUR CONVENIENCE STORE PERPS NEVER HIT A SAFE BEFORE.
IN A WORLD OF DARKNESS...
THE GUNS AREN'T RIGHT, EITHER—THE AUTOMATIC FITS, BUT NOT THE SHOTGUN.

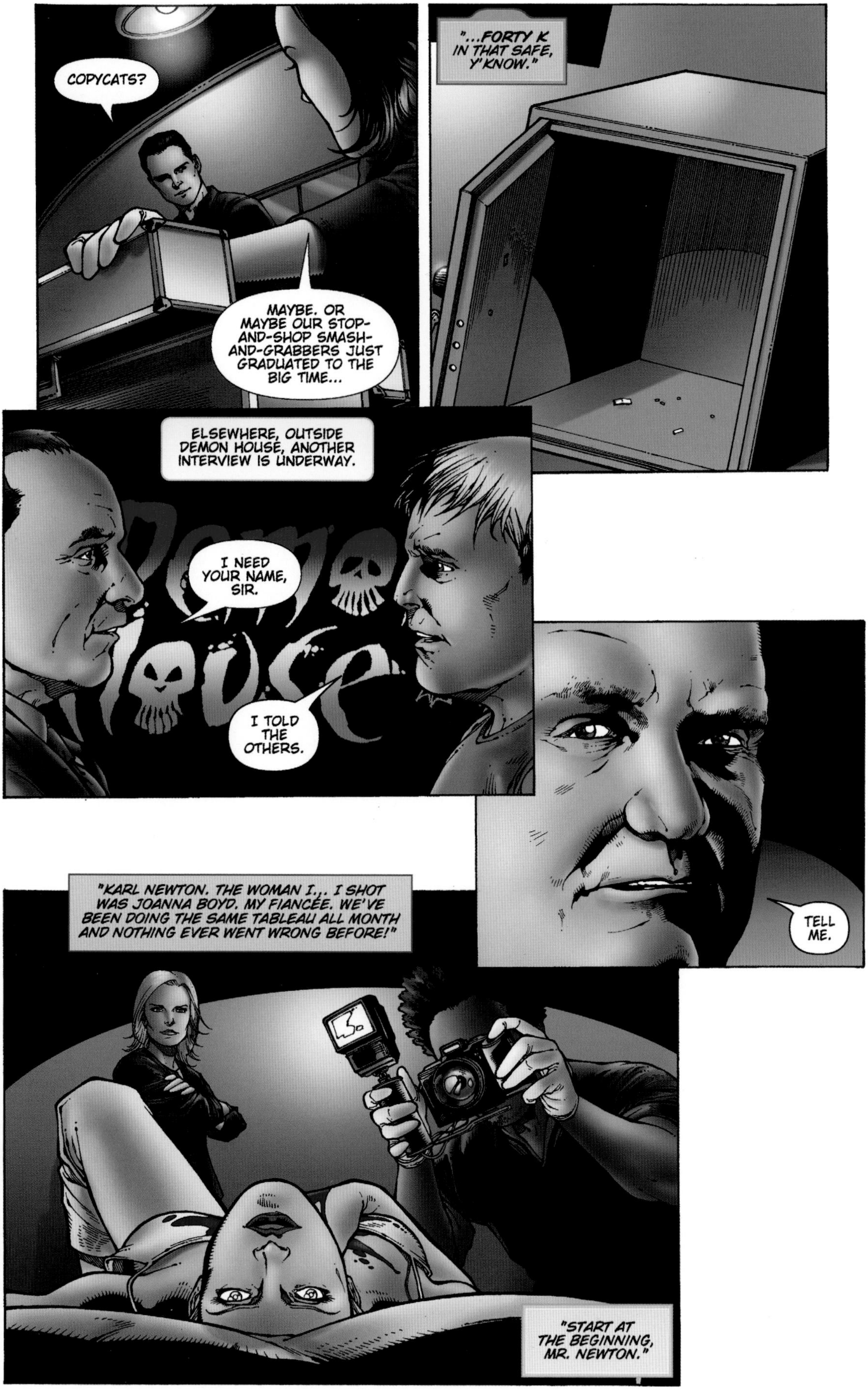

COPYCATS?
MAYBE. OR MAYBE OUR STOP-AND-SHOP SMASH-AND-GRABBERS JUST GRADUATED TO THE BIG TIME...
"...FORTY K IN THAT SAFE, Y'KNOW."
ELSEWHERE, OUTSIDE DEMON HOUSE, ANOTHER INTERVIEW IS UNDERWAY.
I NEED YOUR NAME, SIR.
I TOLD THE OTHERS.
TELL ME.
"KARL NEWTON. THE WOMAN I... I SHOT WAS JOANNA BOYD. MY FIANCÉE. WE'VE BEEN DOING THE SAME TABLEAU ALL MONTH AND NOTHING EVER WENT WRONG BEFORE!"
"START AT THE BEGINNING, MR. NEWTON."

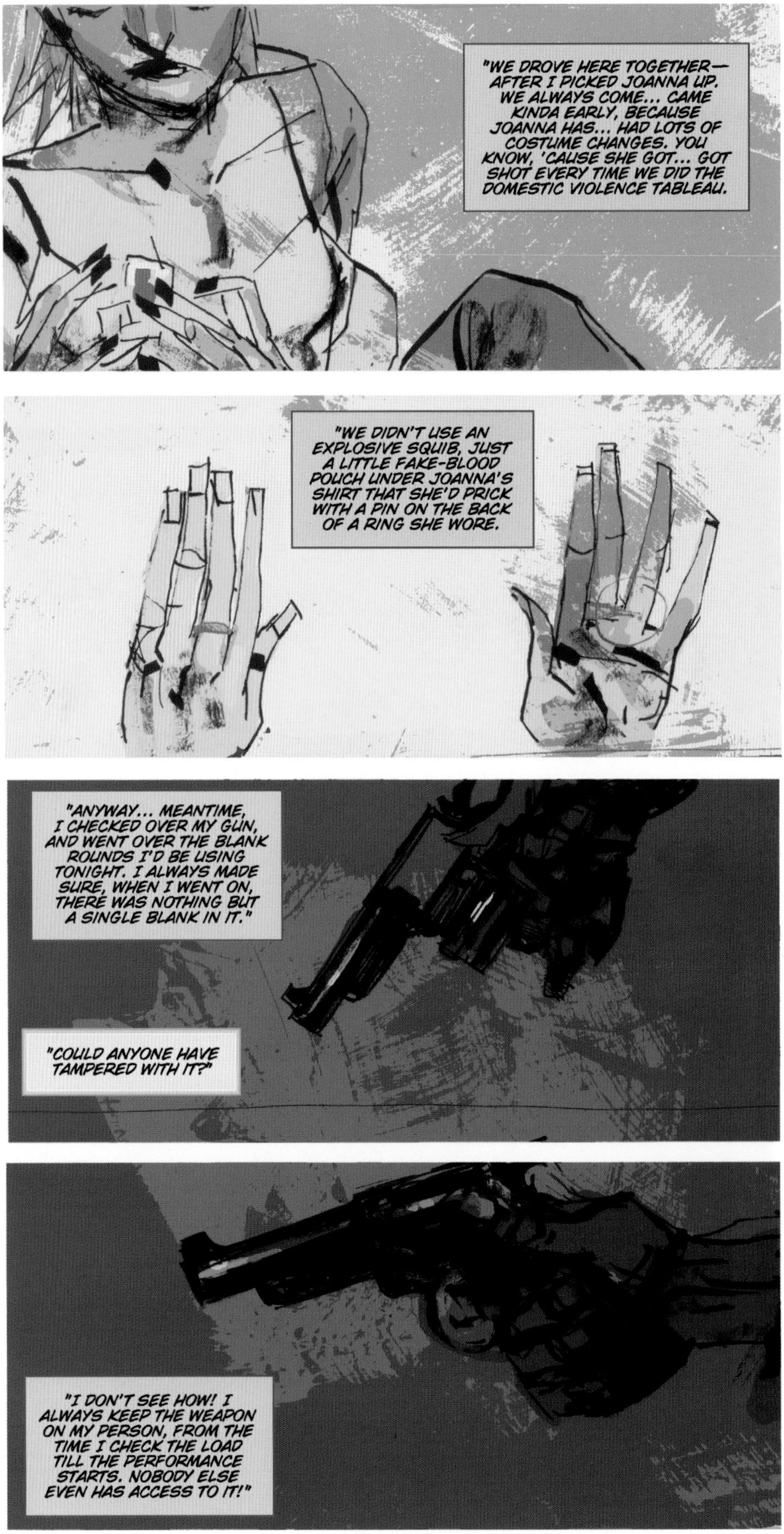
"WE DROVE HERE TOGETHER— AFTER I PICKED JOANNA UP. WE ALWAYS COME... CAME KINDA EARLY, BECAUSE JOANNA HAS... HAD LOTS OF COSTUME CHANGES. YOU KNOW, 'CAUSE SHE GOT... GOT SHOT EVERY TIME WE DID THE DOMESTIC VIOLENCE TABLEAU.
"WE DIDN'T USE AN EXPLOSIVE SQUIB, JUST A LITTLE FAKE-BLOOD POUCH UNDER JOANNA'S SHIRT THAT SHE'D PRICK WITH A PIN ON THE BACK OF A RING SHE WORE.
"ANYWAY... MEANTIME, I CHECKED OVER MY GUN, AND WENT OVER THE BLANK ROUNDS I'D BE USING TONIGHT. I ALWAYS MADE SURE, WHEN I WENT ON, THERE WAS NOTHING BUT A SINGLE BLANK IN IT."
"COULD ANYONE HAVE TAMPERED WITH IT?"
"I DON'T SEE HOW! I ALWAYS KEEP THE WEAPON ON MY PERSON, FROM THE TIME I CHECK THE LOAD TILL THE PERFORMANCE STARTS. NOBODY ELSE EVEN HAS ACCESS TO IT!"

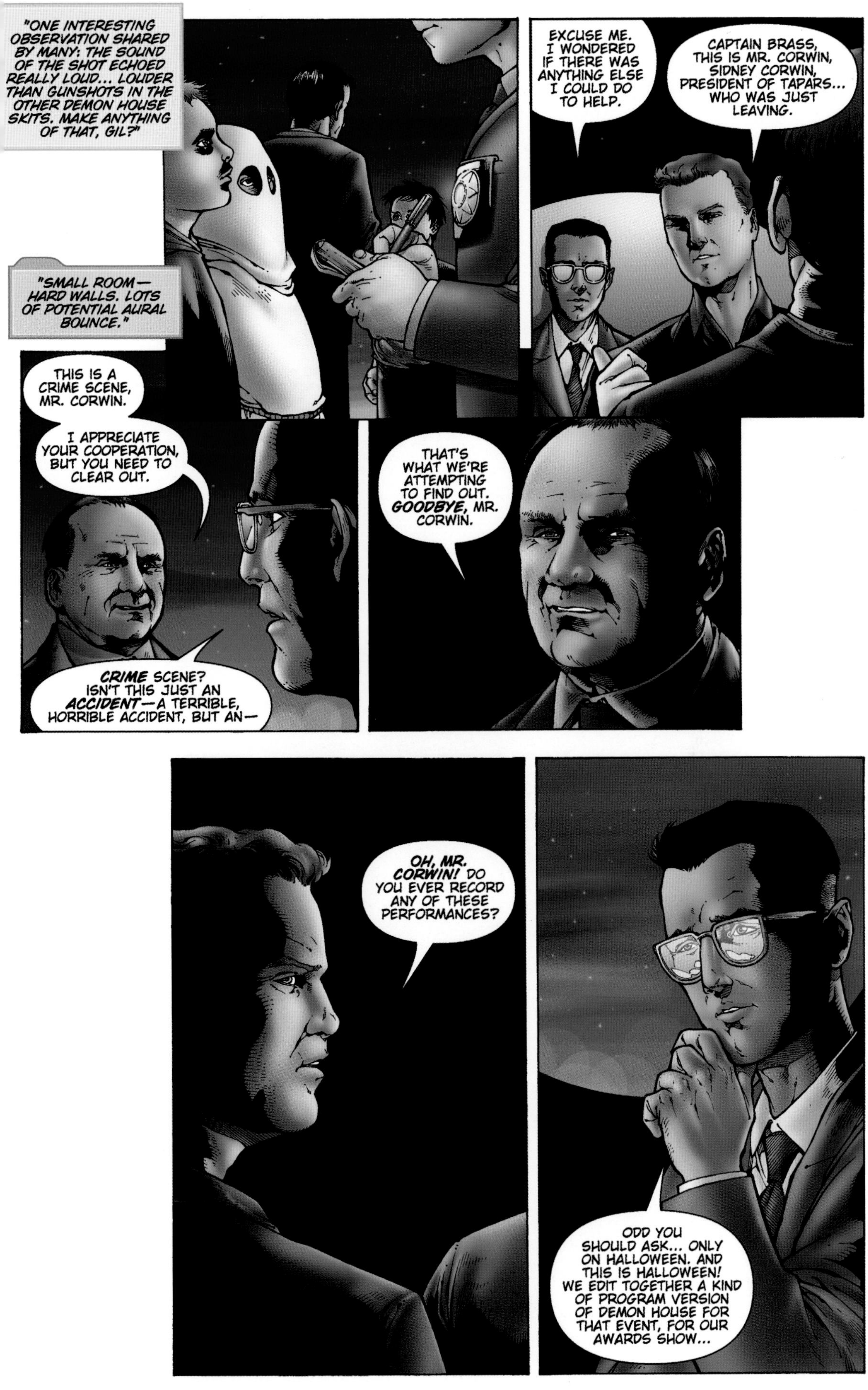
"ONE INTERESTING OBSERVATION SHARED BY MANY: THE SOUND OF THE SHOT ECHOED REALLY LOUD... LOUDER THAN GUNSHOTS IN THE OTHER DEMON HOUSE SKITS. MAKE ANYTHING OF THAT, GIL?"
"SMALL ROOM— HARD WALLS. LOTS OF POTENTIAL AURAL BOUNCE."
EXCUSE ME. I WONDERED IF THERE WAS ANYTHING ELSE I COULD DO TO HELP.
CAPTAIN BRASS, THIS IS MR. CORWIN, SIDNEY CORWIN, PRESIDENT OF TAPARS... WHO WAS JUST LEAVING.
THIS IS A CRIME SCENE, MR. CORWIN.
I APPRECIATE YOUR COOPERATION, BUT YOU NEED TO CLEAR OUT.
CRIME SCENE? ISN'T THIS JUST AN ACCIDENT—A TERRIBLE, HORRIBLE ACCIDENT, BUT AN—
THAT'S WHAT WE'RE ATTEMPTING TO FIND OUT. GOODBYE, MR. CORWIN.
OH, MR. CORWIN! DO YOU EVER RECORD ANY OF THESE PERFORMANCES?
ODD YOU SHOULD ASK... ONLY ON HALLOWEEN. AND THIS IS HALLOWEEN! WE EDIT TOGETHER A KIND OF PROGRAM VERSION OF DEMON HOUSE FOR THAT EVENT, FOR OUR AWARDS SHOW...

Chapter 3
"Curtains for
Joanna"

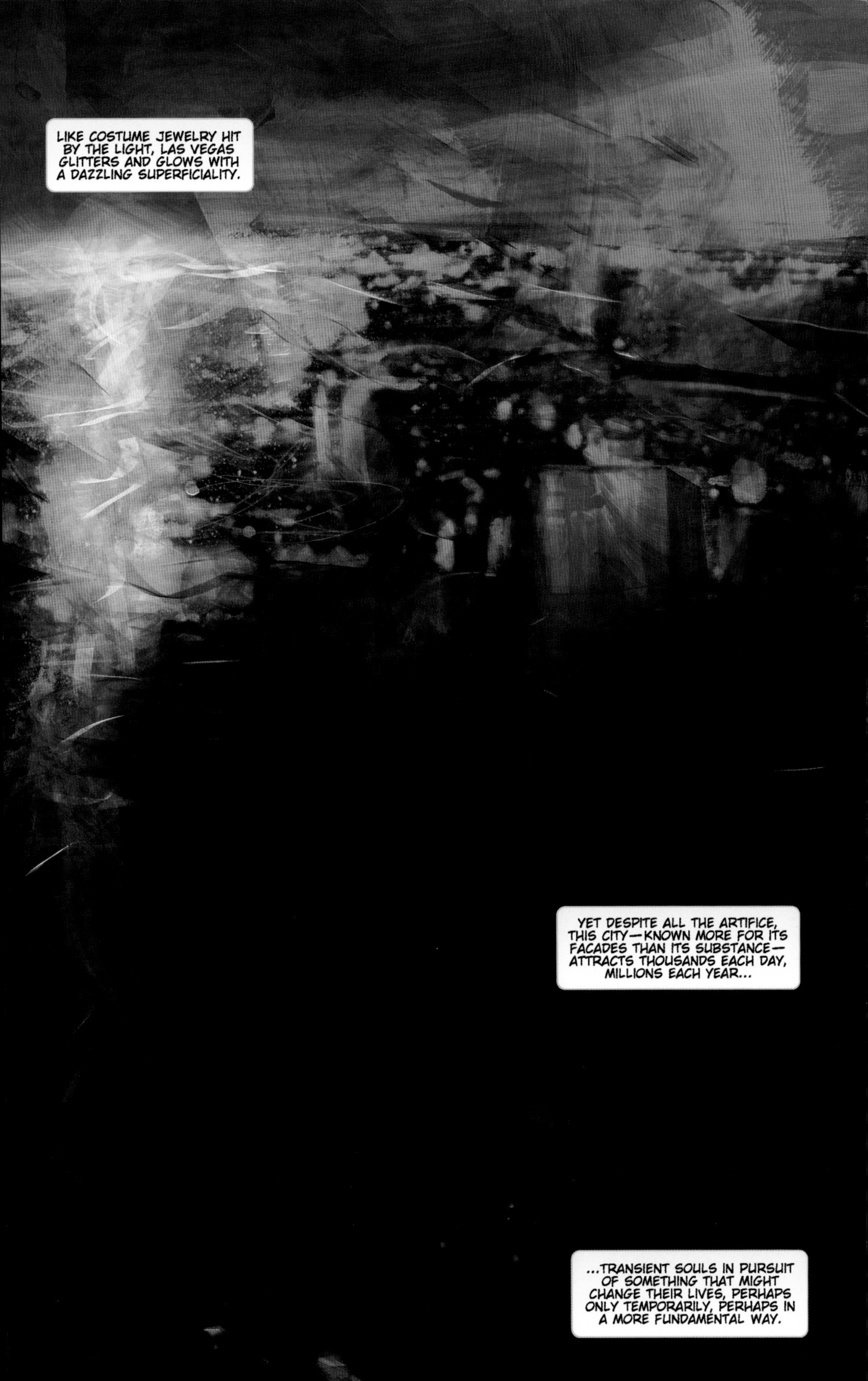
LIKE COSTUME JEWELRY HIT BY THE LIGHT, LAS VEGAS GLITTERS AND GLOWS WITH A DAZZLING SUPERFICIALITY.
YET DESPITE ALL THE ARTIFICE, THIS CITY—KNOWN MORE FOR ITS FACADES THAN ITS SUBSTANCE—ATTRACTS THOUSANDS EACH DAY, MILLIONS EACH YEAR...
...TRANSIENT SOULS IN PURSUIT OF SOMETHING THAT MIGHT CHANGE THEIR LIVES, PERHAPS ONLY TEMPORARILY, PERHAPS IN A MORE FUNDAMENTAL WAY.

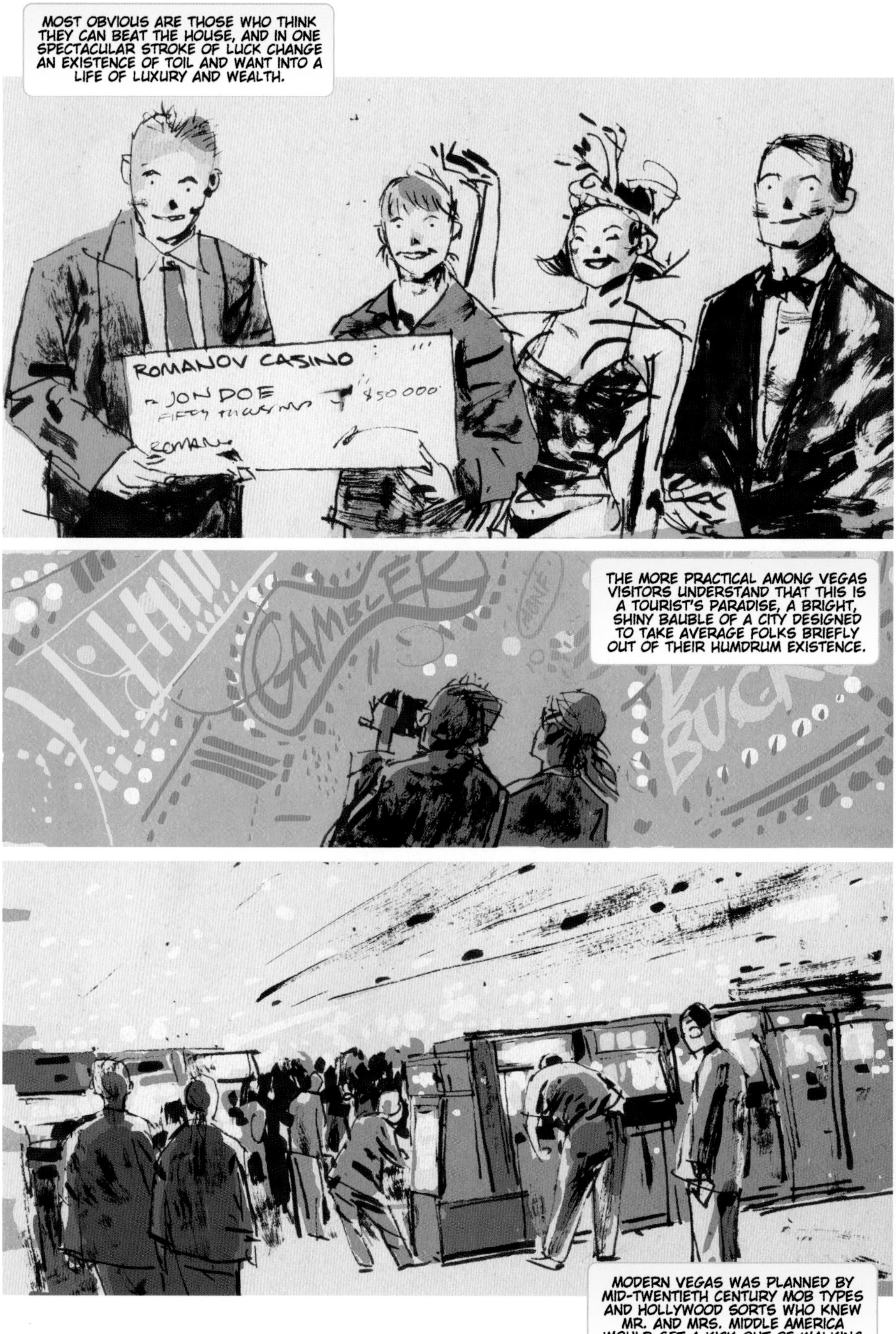
MOST OBVIOUS ARE THOSE WHO THINK THEY CAN BEAT THE HOUSE, AND IN ONE SPECTACULAR STROKE OF LUCK CHANGE AN EXISTENCE OF TOIL AND WANT INTO A LIFE OF LUXURY AND WEALTH.
ROMANOV CASINO
JON DOE
$50 000
THE MORE PRACTICAL AMONG VEGAS VISITORS UNDERSTAND THAT THIS IS A TOURIST'S PARADISE, A BRIGHT, SHINY BAUBLE OF A CITY DESIGNED TO TAKE AVERAGE FOLKS BRIEFLY OUT OF THEIR HUMDRUM EXISTENCE.
GAMBLER
MODERN VEGAS WAS PLANNED BY MID-TWENTIETH CENTURY MOB TYPES AND HOLLYWOOD SORTS WHO KNEW MR. AND MRS. MIDDLE AMERICA WOULD GET A KICK OUT OF WALKING INTO A REAL-LIFE MOVIE SET.

BUT THE NEON OASIS IN THE NEVADA DESERT IS MORE THAN JUST TOPLESS REVUES, CHEAP BUFFETS, AND FREE PARKING—FOR DECADES, IT'S BEEN ONE OF AMERICA'S FAST-GROWING CITIES.

OVER FOUR THOUSAND COME TO THIS SECOND-CHANCE CITY EVERY MONTH... PEOPLE WHO WANT A PERMANENT CHANGE—THE KIND YOU DON'T GET FROM A THREE-DAY JUNKET OR WEEK-LONG VACATION.

AMERICA'S DREAM FACTORY FOR VISITORS IS A WORKING-CLASS TOWN FOR ITS INHABITANTS. TAXES ARE LOW, BUT TEMPTATIONS HIGH...

...THE CITIZENS OF LAS VEGAS SMOKE AND DRINK AND, YES, GAMBLE MORE THAN THEIR COUNTERPARTS IN OTHER CITIES... AND THEIR SUICIDE RATE IS TWICE THE NATIONAL AVERAGE.

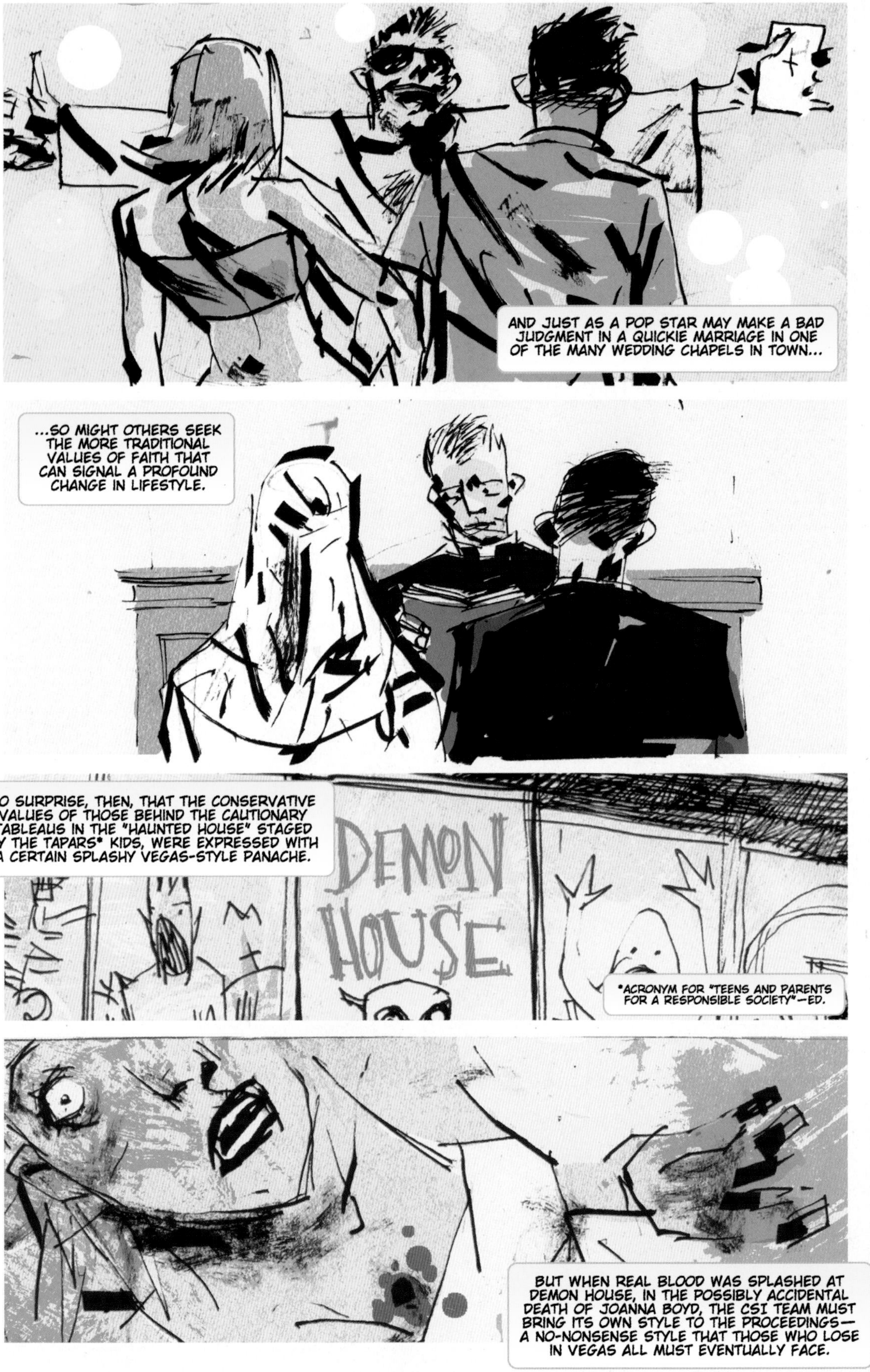
AND JUST AS A POP STAR MAY MAKE A BAD JUDGMENT IN A QUICKIE MARRIAGE IN ONE OF THE MANY WEDDING CHAPELS IN TOWN...
...SO MIGHT OTHERS SEEK THE MORE TRADITIONAL VALUES OF FAITH THAT CAN SIGNAL A PROFOUND CHANGE IN LIFESTYLE.
NO SURPRISE, THEN, THAT THE CONSERVATIVE VALUES OF THOSE BEHIND THE CAUTIONARY TABLEAUS IN THE "HAUNTED HOUSE" STAGED BY THE TAPARS* KIDS, WERE EXPRESSED WITH A CERTAIN SPLASHY VEGAS-STYLE PANACHE.
DEMON HOUSE
*ACRONYM FOR "TEENS AND PARENTS FOR A RESPONSIBLE SOCIETY"—ED.
BUT WHEN REAL BLOOD WAS SPLASHED AT DEMON HOUSE, IN THE POSSIBLY ACCIDENTAL DEATH OF JOANNA BOYD, THE CSI TEAM MUST BRING ITS OWN STYLE TO THE PROCEEDINGS—A NO-NONSENSE STYLE THAT THOSE WHO LOSE IN VEGAS ALL MUST EVENTUALLY FACE.

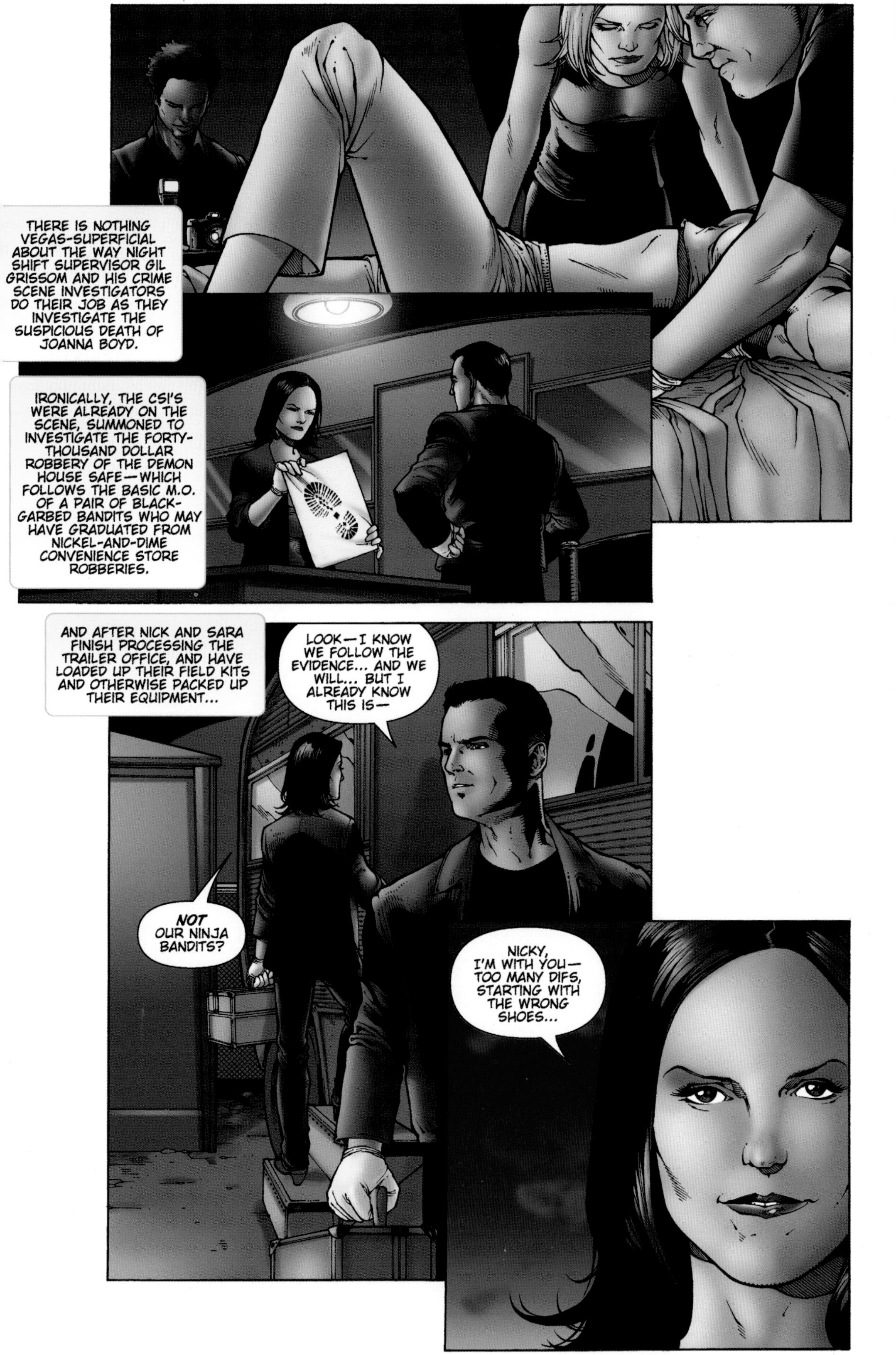
THERE IS NOTHING VEGAS-SUPERFICIAL ABOUT THE WAY NIGHT SHIFT SUPERVISOR GIL GRISSOM AND HIS CRIME SCENE INVESTIGATORS DO THEIR JOB AS THEY INVESTIGATE THE SUSPICIOUS DEATH OF JOANNA BOYD.
IRONICALLY, THE CSI'S WERE ALREADY ON THE SCENE, SUMMONED TO INVESTIGATE THE FORTY-THOUSAND DOLLAR ROBBERY OF THE DEMON HOUSE SAFE—WHICH FOLLOWS THE BASIC M.O. OF A PAIR OF BLACK-GARBED BANDITS WHO MAY HAVE GRADUATED FROM NICKEL-AND-DIME CONVENIENCE STORE ROBBERIES.
AND AFTER NICK AND SARA FINISH PROCESSING THE TRAILER OFFICE, AND HAVE LOADED UP THEIR FIELD KITS AND OTHERWISE PACKED UP THEIR EQUIPMENT...
LOOK—I KNOW WE FOLLOW THE EVIDENCE... AND WE WILL... BUT I ALREADY KNOW THIS IS—
NOT OUR NINJA BANDITS?
NICKY, I'M WITH YOU—TOO MANY DIFS, STARTING WITH THE WRONG SHOES...

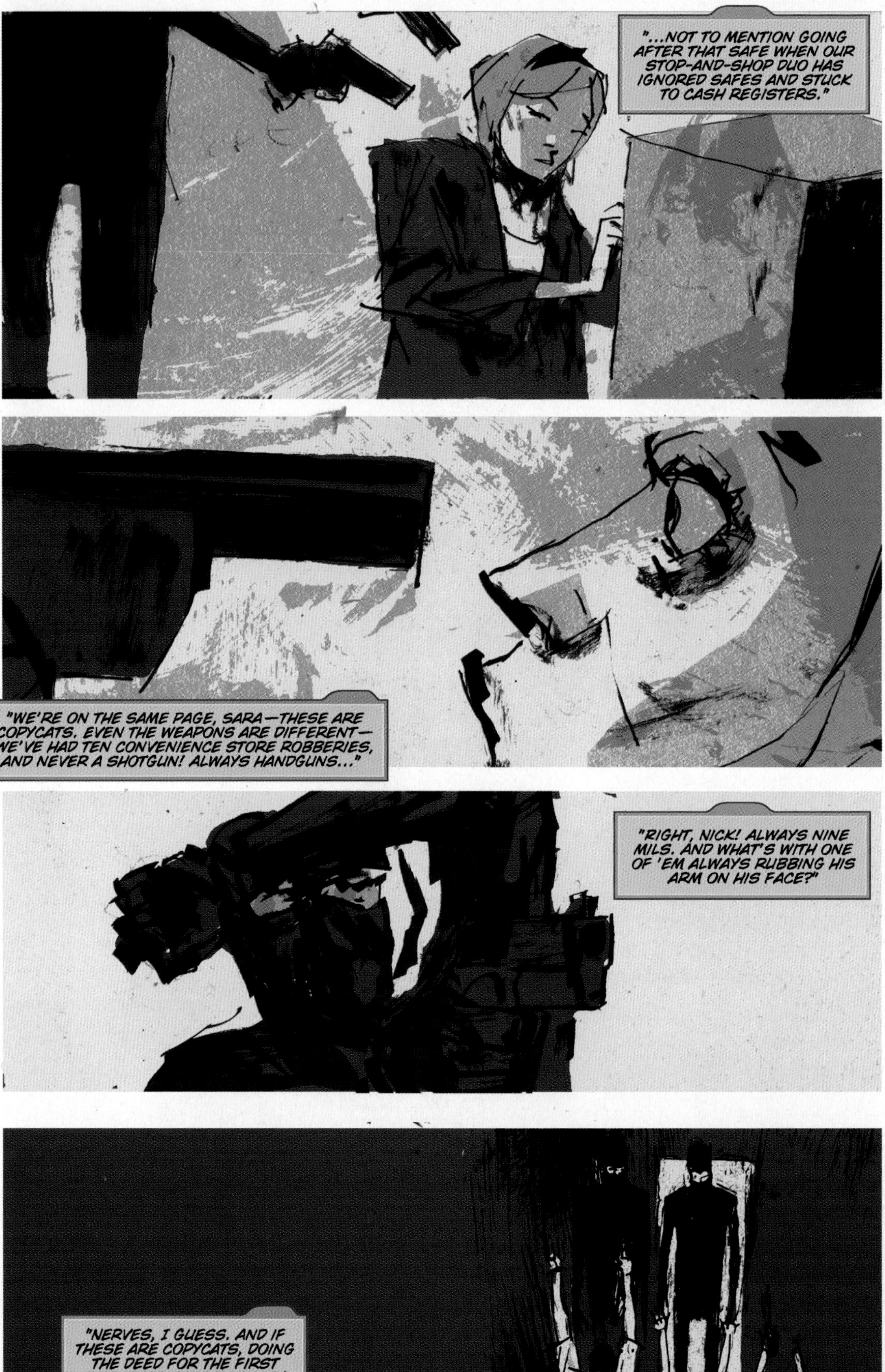
"...NOT TO MENTION GOING AFTER THAT SAFE WHEN OUR STOP-AND-SHOP DUO HAS IGNORED SAFES AND STUCK TO CASH REGISTERS."
"WE'RE ON THE SAME PAGE, SARA—THESE ARE COPYCATS. EVEN THE WEAPONS ARE DIFFERENT—WE'VE HAD TEN CONVENIENCE STORE ROBBERIES, AND NEVER A SHOTGUN! ALWAYS HANDGUNS..."
"RIGHT, NICK! ALWAYS NINE MILS. AND WHAT'S WITH ONE OF 'EM ALWAYS RUBBING HIS ARM ON HIS FACE?"
"NERVES, I GUESS. AND IF THESE ARE COPYCATS, DOING THE DEED FOR THE FIRST TIME, THAT MAKES SENSE."

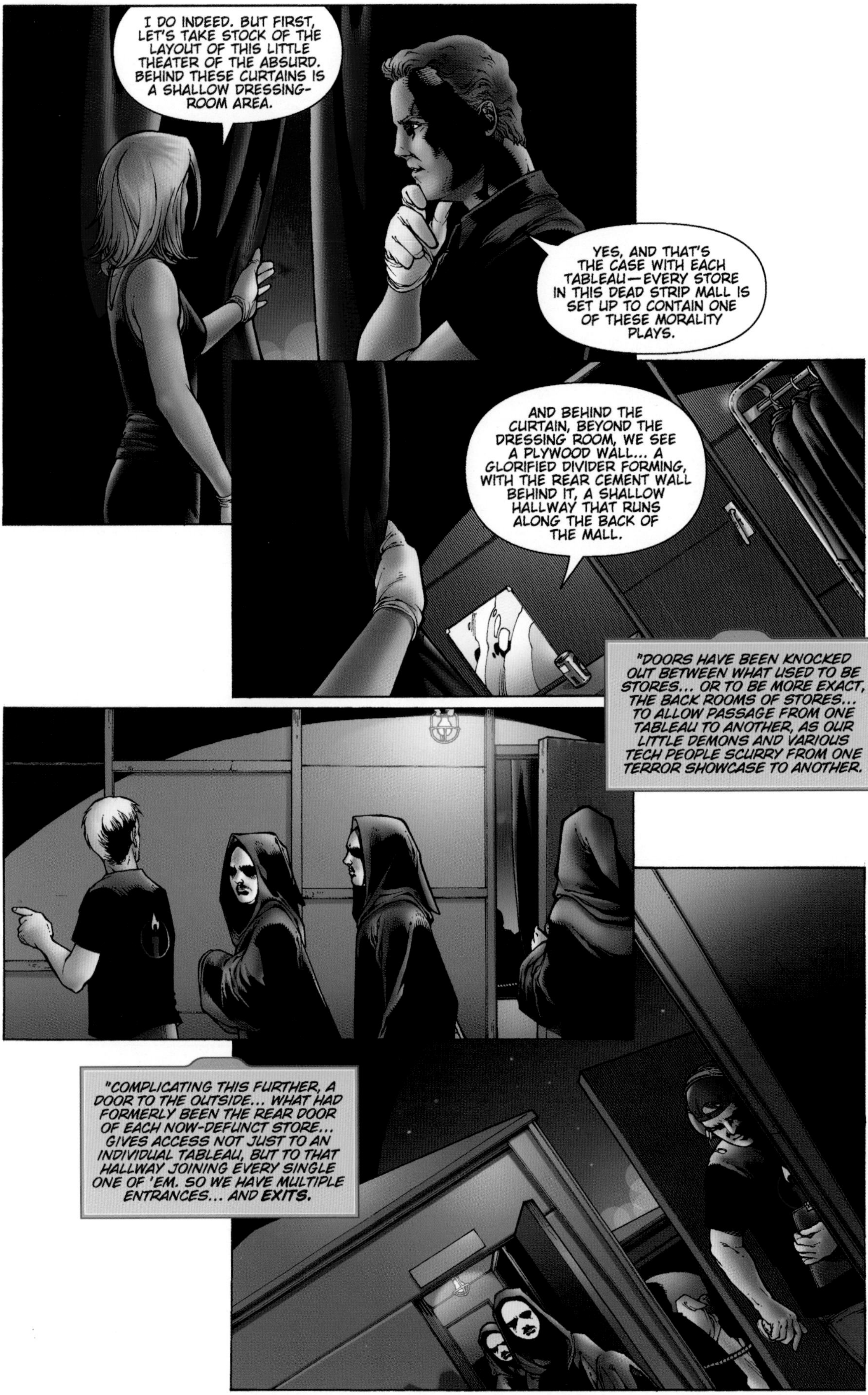
I DO INDEED. BUT FIRST, LET'S TAKE STOCK OF THE LAYOUT OF THIS LITTLE THEATER OF THE ABSURD. BEHIND THESE CURTAINS IS A SHALLOW DRESSING-ROOM AREA.
YES, AND THAT'S THE CASE WITH EACH TABLEAU—EVERY STORE IN THIS DEAD STRIP MALL IS SET UP TO CONTAIN ONE OF THESE MORALITY PLAYS.
AND BEHIND THE CURTAIN, BEYOND THE DRESSING ROOM, WE SEE A PLYWOOD WALL... A GLORIFIED DIVIDER FORMING, WITH THE REAR CEMENT WALL BEHIND IT, A SHALLOW HALLWAY THAT RUNS ALONG THE BACK OF THE MALL.
"DOORS HAVE BEEN KNOCKED OUT BETWEEN WHAT USED TO BE STORES... OR TO BE MORE EXACT, THE BACK ROOMS OF STORES... TO ALLOW PASSAGE FROM ONE TABLEAU TO ANOTHER, AS OUR LITTLE DEMONS AND VARIOUS TECH PEOPLE SCURRY FROM ONE TERROR SHOWCASE TO ANOTHER.
"COMPLICATING THIS FURTHER, A DOOR TO THE OUTSIDE... WHAT HAD FORMERLY BEEN THE REAR DOOR OF EACH NOW-DEFUNCT STORE... GIVES ACCESS NOT JUST TO AN INDIVIDUAL TABLEAU, BUT TO THAT HALLWAY JOINING EVERY SINGLE ONE OF 'EM. SO WE HAVE MULTIPLE ENTRANCES... AND EXITS.

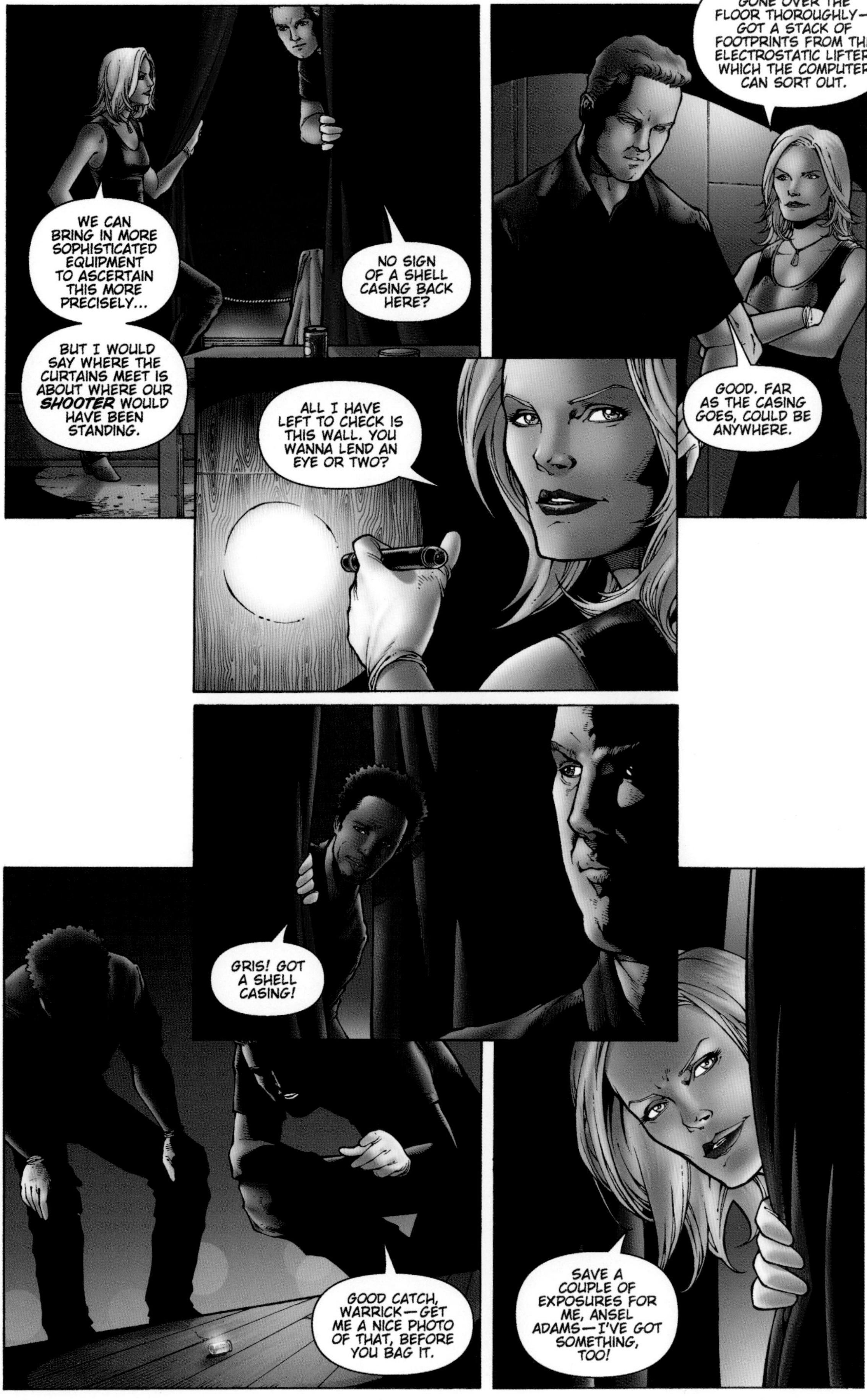
WE CAN BRING IN MORE SOPHISTICATED EQUIPMENT TO ASCERTAIN THIS MORE PRECISELY...
BUT I WOULD SAY WHERE THE CURTAINS MEET IS ABOUT WHERE OUR SHOOTER WOULD HAVE BEEN STANDING.
NO SIGN OF A SHELL CASING BACK HERE?
NO, AND I'VE GONE OVER THE FLOOR THOROUGHLY—GOT A STACK OF FOOTPRINTS FROM THE ELECTROSTATIC LIFTER, WHICH THE COMPUTER CAN SORT OUT.
GOOD. FAR AS THE CASING GOES, COULD BE ANYWHERE.
ALL I HAVE LEFT TO CHECK IS THIS WALL. YOU WANNA LEND AN EYE OR TWO?
GRIS! GOT A SHELL CASING!
GOOD CATCH, WARRICK—GET ME A NICE PHOTO OF THAT, BEFORE YOU BAG IT.
SAVE A COUPLE OF EXPOSURES FOR ME, ANSEL ADAMS—I'VE GOT SOMETHING, TOO!

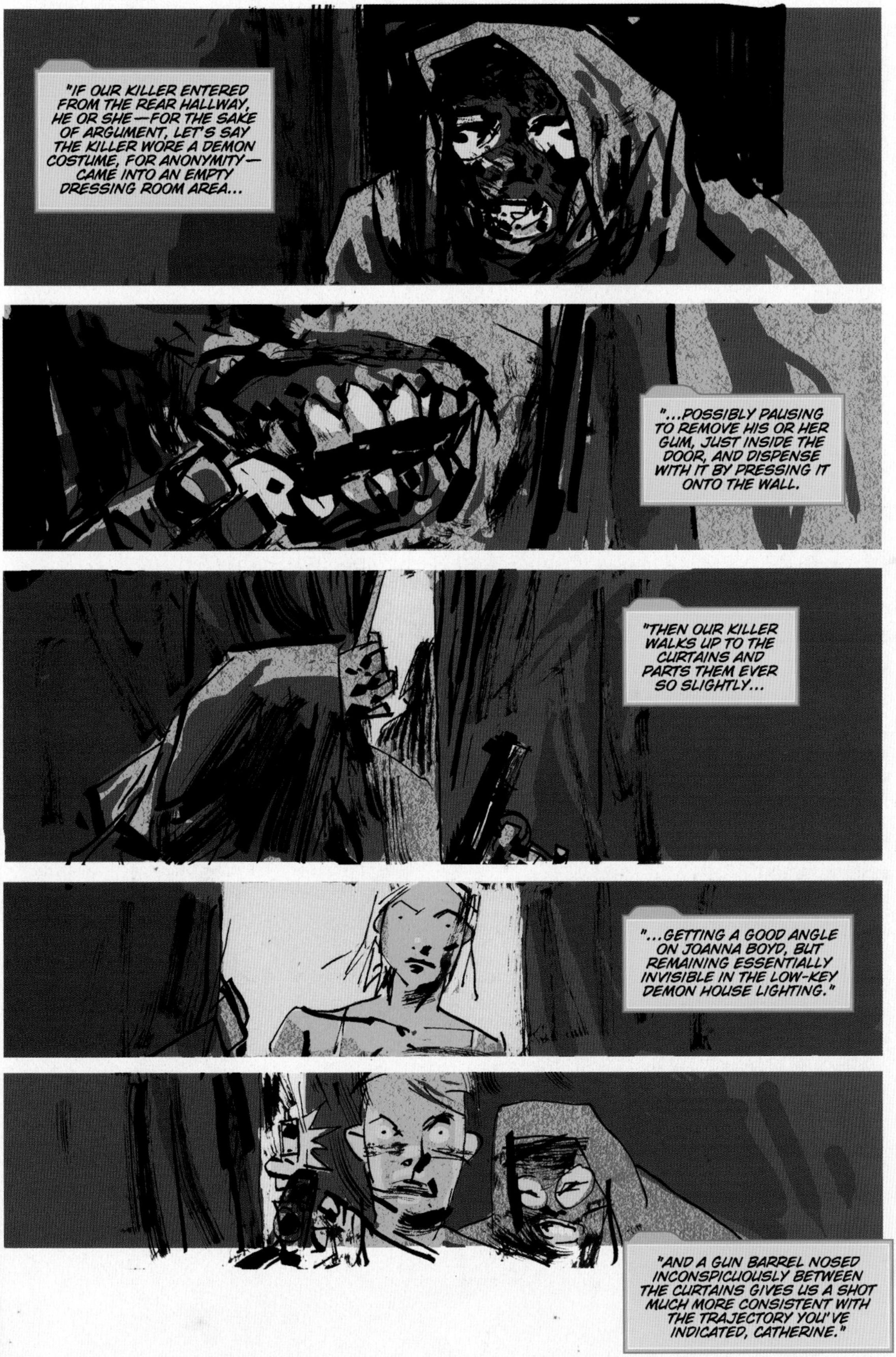
"IF OUR KILLER ENTERED FROM THE REAR HALLWAY, HE OR SHE—FOR THE SAKE OF ARGUMENT, LET'S SAY THE KILLER WORE A DEMON COSTUME, FOR ANONYMITY—CAME INTO AN EMPTY DRESSING ROOM AREA...
"...POSSIBLY PAUSING TO REMOVE HIS OR HER GUM, JUST INSIDE THE DOOR, AND DISPENSE WITH IT BY PRESSING IT ONTO THE WALL.
"THEN OUR KILLER WALKS UP TO THE CURTAINS AND PARTS THEM EVER SO SLIGHTLY...
"...GETTING A GOOD ANGLE ON JOANNA BOYD, BUT REMAINING ESSENTIALLY INVISIBLE IN THE LOW-KEY DEMON HOUSE LIGHTING."
"AND A GUN BARREL NOSED INCONSPICUOUSLY BETWEEN THE CURTAINS GIVES US A SHOT MUCH MORE CONSISTENT WITH THE TRAJECTORY YOU'VE INDICATED, CATHERINE."

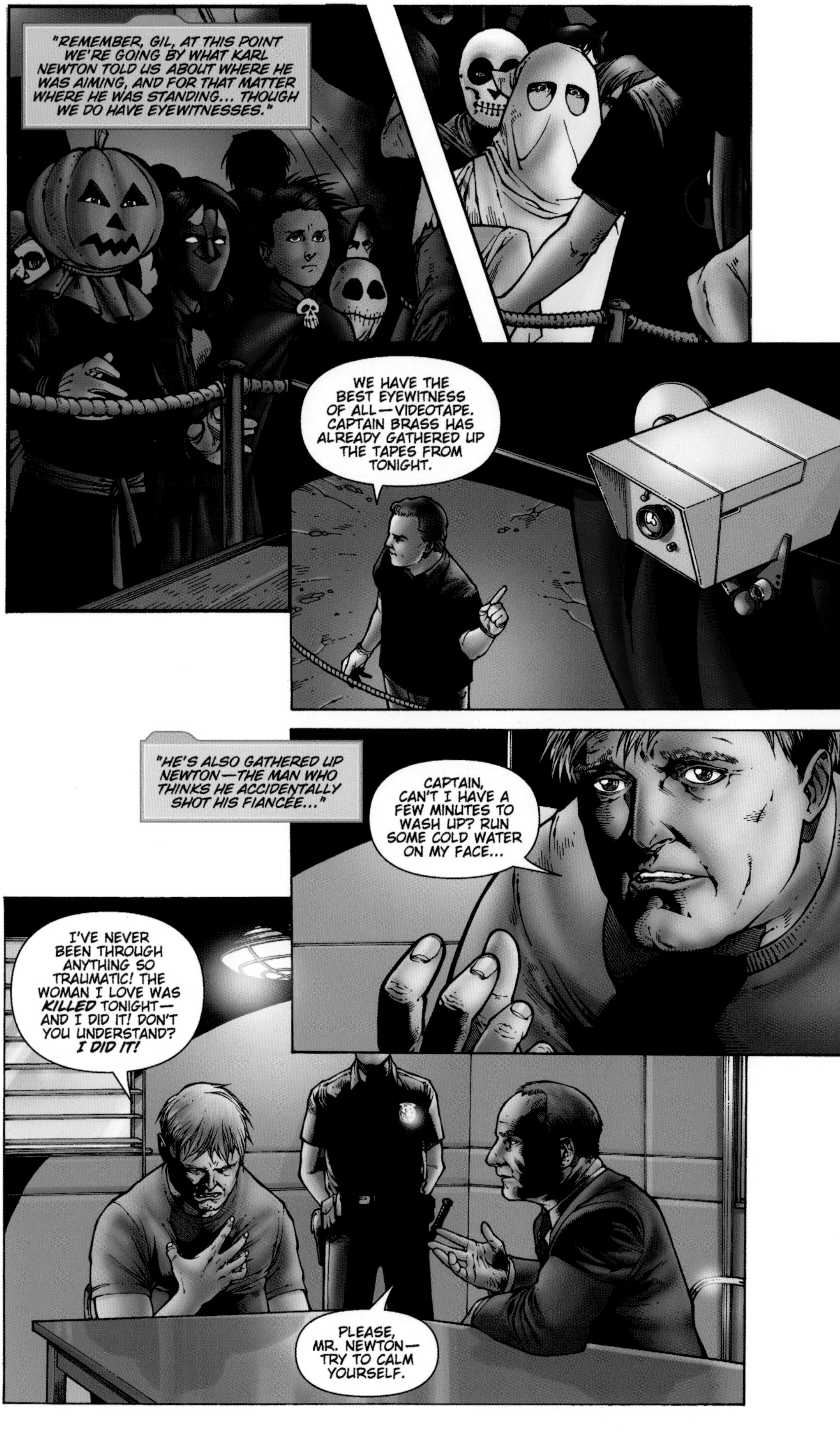
"REMEMBER, GIL, AT THIS POINT WE'RE GOING BY WHAT KARL NEWTON TOLD US ABOUT WHERE HE WAS AIMING, AND FOR THAT MATTER WHERE HE WAS STANDING... THOUGH WE DO HAVE EYEWITNESSES."
WE HAVE THE BEST EYEWITNESS OF ALL—VIDEOTAPE. CAPTAIN BRASS HAS ALREADY GATHERED UP THE TAPES FROM TONIGHT.
"HE'S ALSO GATHERED UP NEWTON—THE MAN WHO THINKS HE ACCIDENTALLY SHOT HIS FIANCÉE..."
CAPTAIN, CAN'T I HAVE A FEW MINUTES TO WASH UP? RUN SOME COLD WATER ON MY FACE...
I'VE NEVER BEEN THROUGH ANYTHING SO TRAUMATIC! THE WOMAN I LOVE WAS KILLED TONIGHT—AND I DID IT! DON'T YOU UNDERSTAND? I DID IT!
PLEASE, MR. NEWTON—TRY TO CALM YOURSELF.

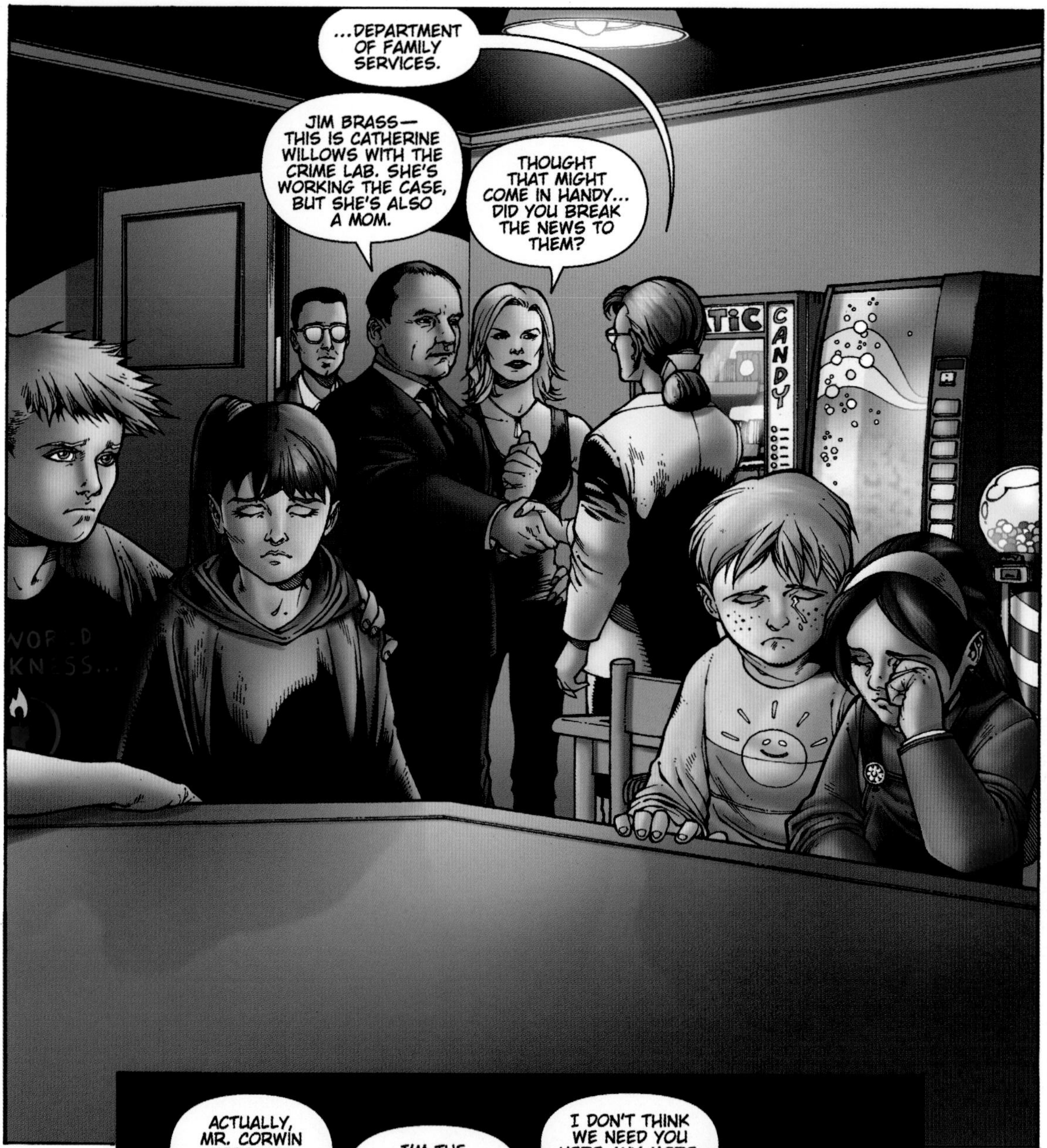
...DEPARTMENT OF FAMILY SERVICES.
JIM BRASS— THIS IS CATHERINE WILLOWS WITH THE CRIME LAB. SHE'S WORKING THE CASE, BUT SHE'S ALSO A MOM.
THOUGHT THAT MIGHT COME IN HANDY... DID YOU BREAK THE NEWS TO THEM?
CANDY

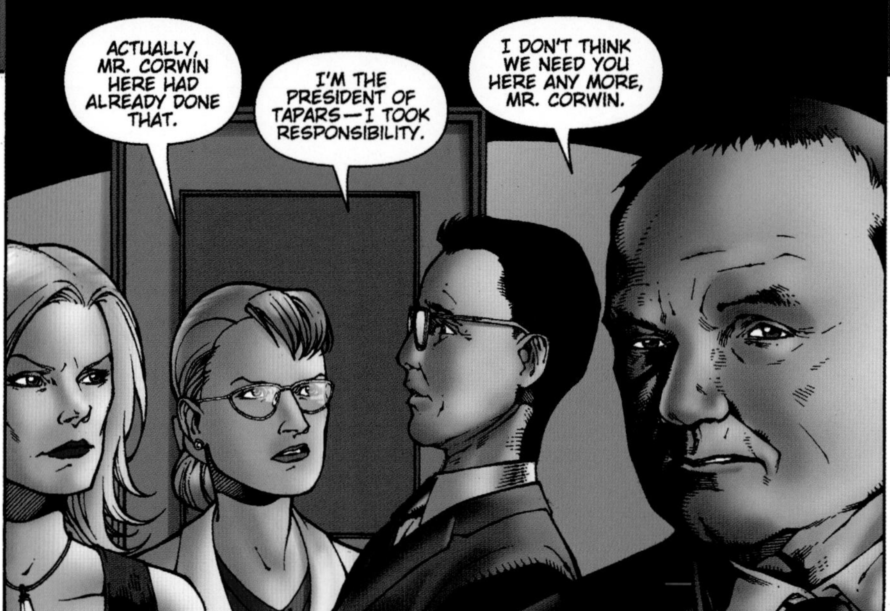
ACTUALLY, MR. CORWIN HERE HAD ALREADY DONE THAT.
I'M THE PRESIDENT OF TAPARS—I TOOK RESPONSIBILITY.
I DON'T THINK WE NEED YOU HERE ANY MORE, MR. CORWIN.

"CAPTAIN BRASS, MS. WILLOWS—THE TEENS ARE RUTH AND MARK NEWTON... FOURTEEN AND SIXTEEN, RESPECTIVELY. THE YOUNGER ONES ARE BRIAN AND DIANA BOYD... SIX AND EIGHT.

WITH YOUR PERMISSION, I'D LIKE TO TURN THESE YOUNG ONES OVER TO AN ASSOCIATE WHO'S WAITING FOR THEM TO BE TAKEN DIRECTLY TO A FOSTER HOME—UNLESS YOU HAVE QUESTIONS FOR THEM.

PLEASE.

AFTER BRIEF INTRODUCTIONS, BRASS TAKES THE LEAD.

WE'RE SORRY FOR YOUR LOSS, BUT WE'D LIKE YOU TO HELP US...

WHERE THE HELL HAVE YOU TAKEN MY DAD? I SAW YOU PUT HIM IN A SQUAD CAR!

BUT HE *IS* AT THE POLICE STATION! YOU DID TAKE HIM AWAY, RIGHT? *WHY?* WASN'T THIS AN *ACCIDENT?*

YOUR FATHER ISN'T UNDER ARREST. HE'S HELPING US FIGURE OUT WHAT HAPPENED TONIGHT.

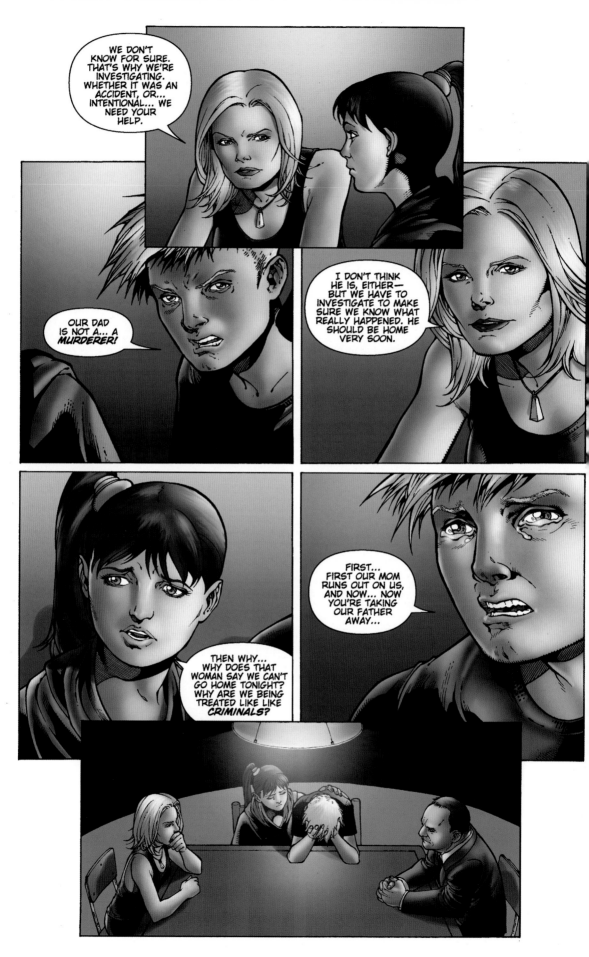

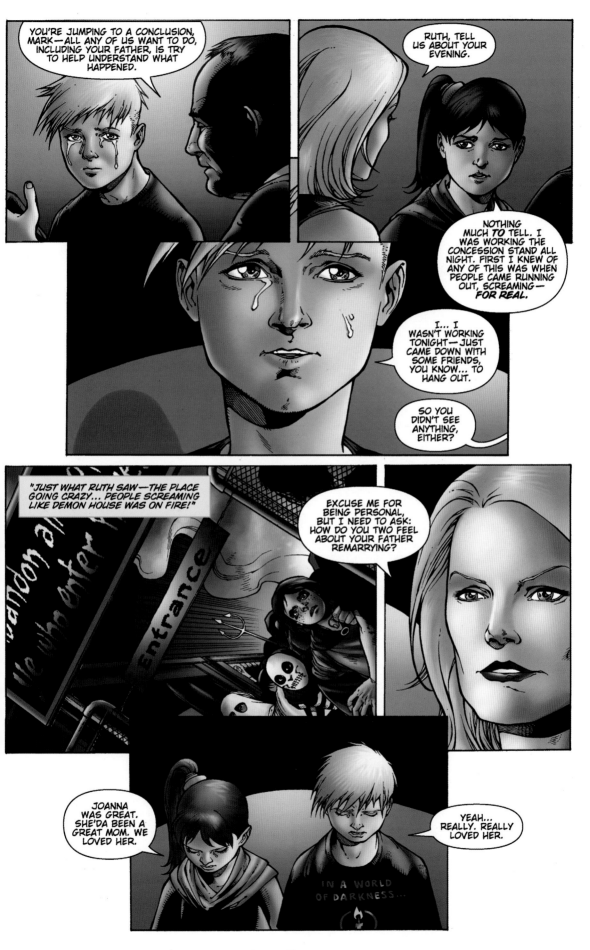

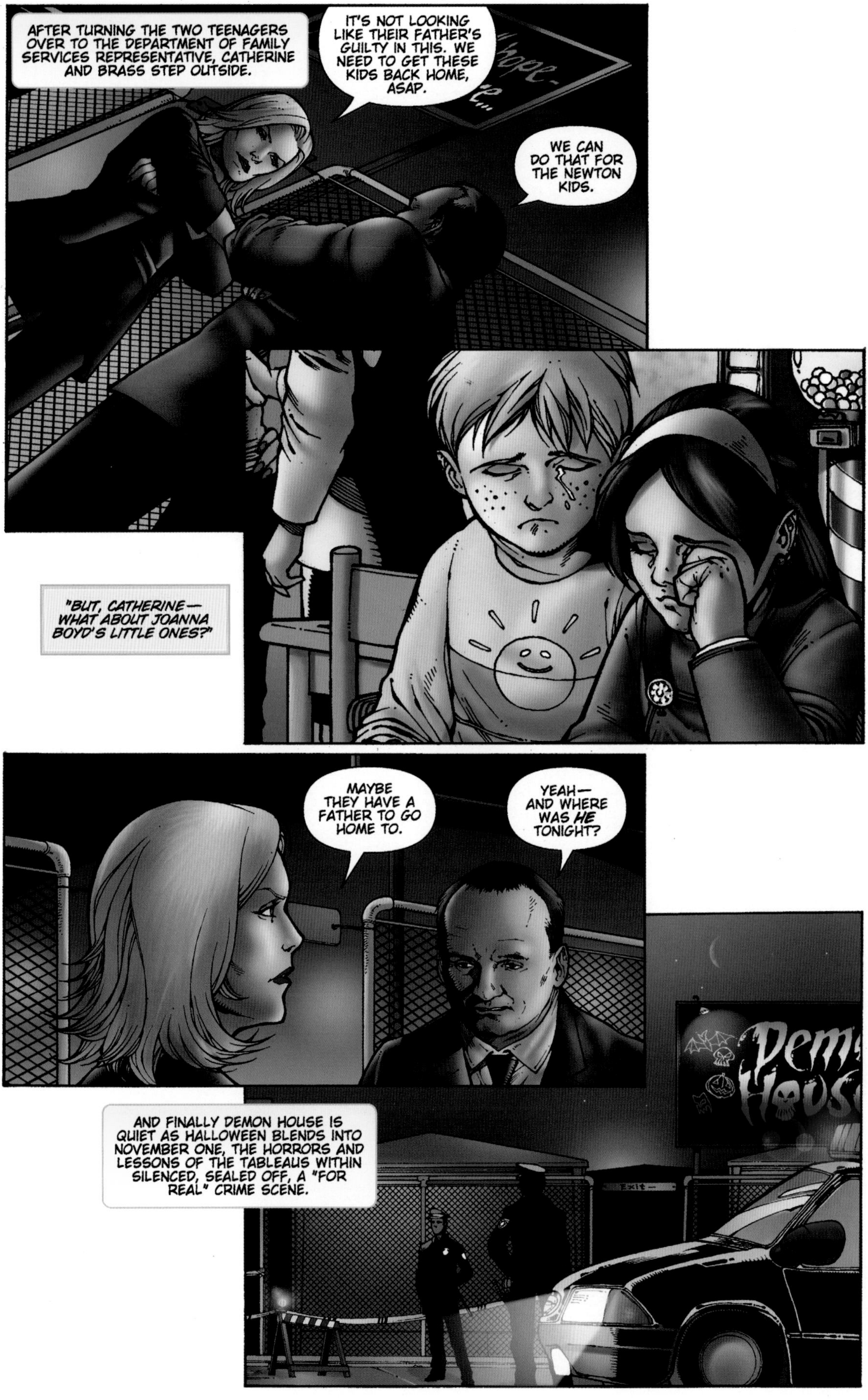

AFTER TURNING THE TWO TEENAGERS OVER TO THE DEPARTMENT OF FAMILY SERVICES REPRESENTATIVE, CATHERINE AND BRASS STEP OUTSIDE.
IT'S NOT LOOKING LIKE THEIR FATHER'S GUILTY IN THIS. WE NEED TO GET THESE KIDS BACK HOME, ASAP.
WE CAN DO THAT FOR THE NEWTON KIDS.
"BUT, CATHERINE— WHAT ABOUT JOANNA BOYD'S LITTLE ONES?"
MAYBE THEY HAVE A FATHER TO GO HOME TO.
YEAH— AND WHERE WAS *HE* TONIGHT?
AND FINALLY DEMON HOUSE IS QUIET AS HALLOWEEN BLENDS INTO NOVEMBER ONE, THE HORRORS AND LESSONS OF THE TABLEAUS WITHIN SILENCED, SEALED OFF, A "FOR REAL" CRIME SCENE.

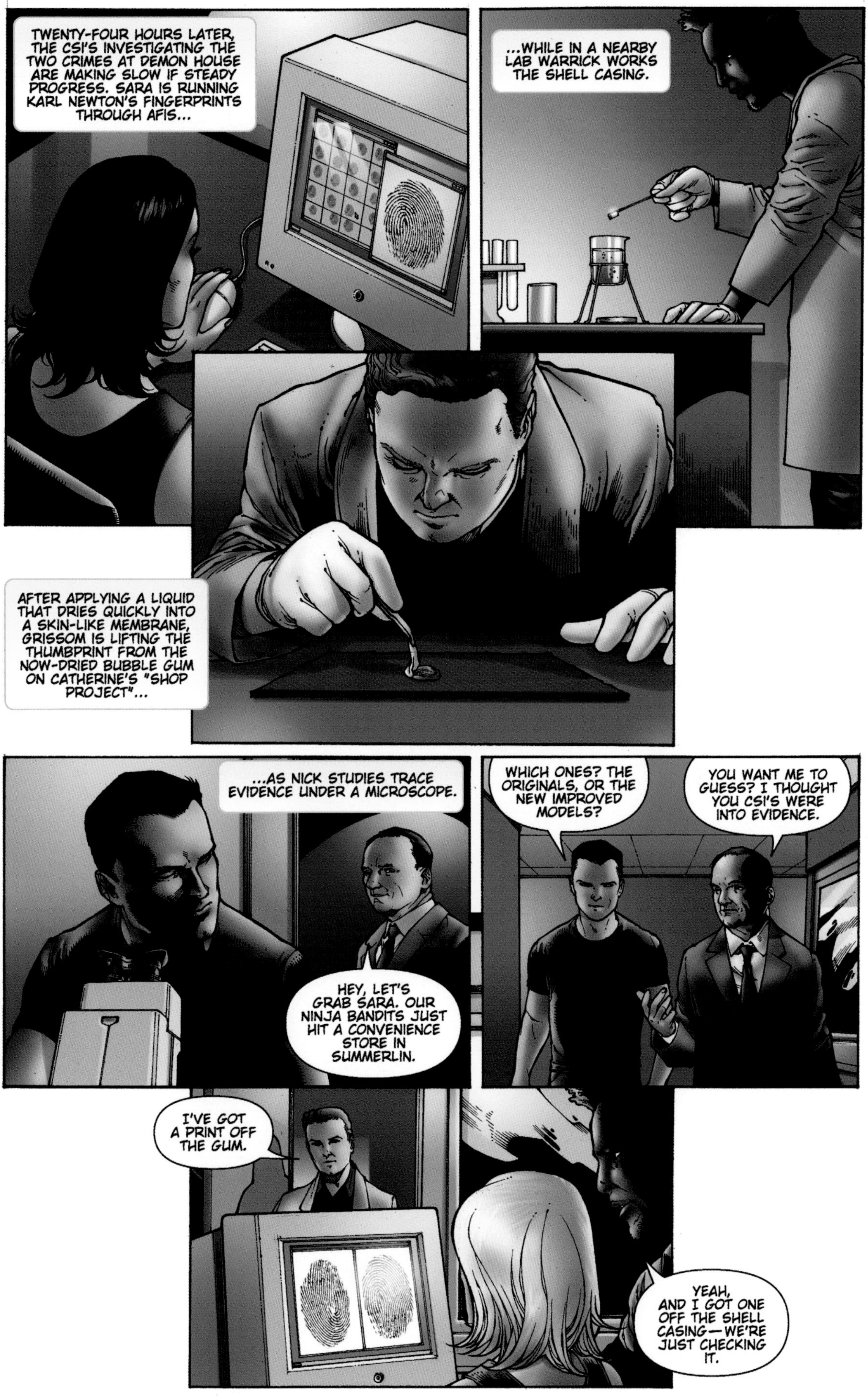
TWENTY-FOUR HOURS LATER, THE CSI'S INVESTIGATING THE TWO CRIMES AT DEMON HOUSE ARE MAKING SLOW IF STEADY PROGRESS. SARA IS RUNNING KARL NEWTON'S FINGERPRINTS THROUGH AFIS...
...WHILE IN A NEARBY LAB WARRICK WORKS THE SHELL CASING.
AFTER APPLYING A LIQUID THAT DRIES QUICKLY INTO A SKIN-LIKE MEMBRANE, GRISSOM IS LIFTING THE THUMBPRINT FROM THE NOW-DRIED BUBBLE GUM ON CATHERINE'S "SHOP PROJECT"...
...AS NICK STUDIES TRACE EVIDENCE UNDER A MICROSCOPE.
HEY, LET'S GRAB SARA. OUR NINJA BANDITS JUST HIT A CONVENIENCE STORE IN SUMMERLIN.
WHICH ONES? THE ORIGINALS, OR THE NEW IMPROVED MODELS?
YOU WANT ME TO GUESS? I THOUGHT YOU CSI'S WERE INTO EVIDENCE.
I'VE GOT A PRINT OFF THE GUM.
YEAH, AND I GOT ONE OFF THE SHELL CASING—WE'RE JUST CHECKING IT.

Chapter 4

"Quarterback Sneak"

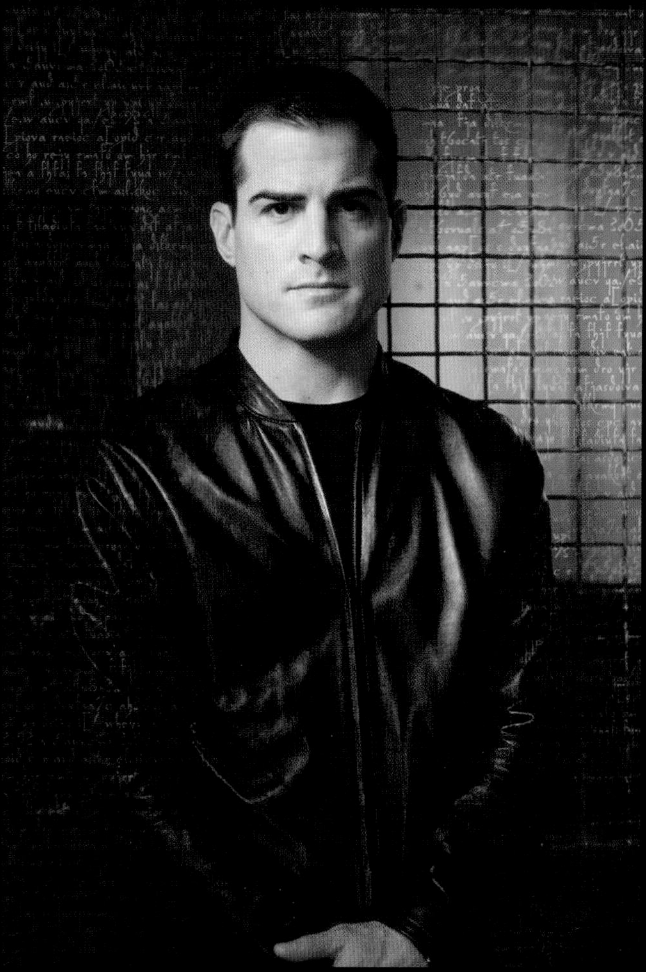

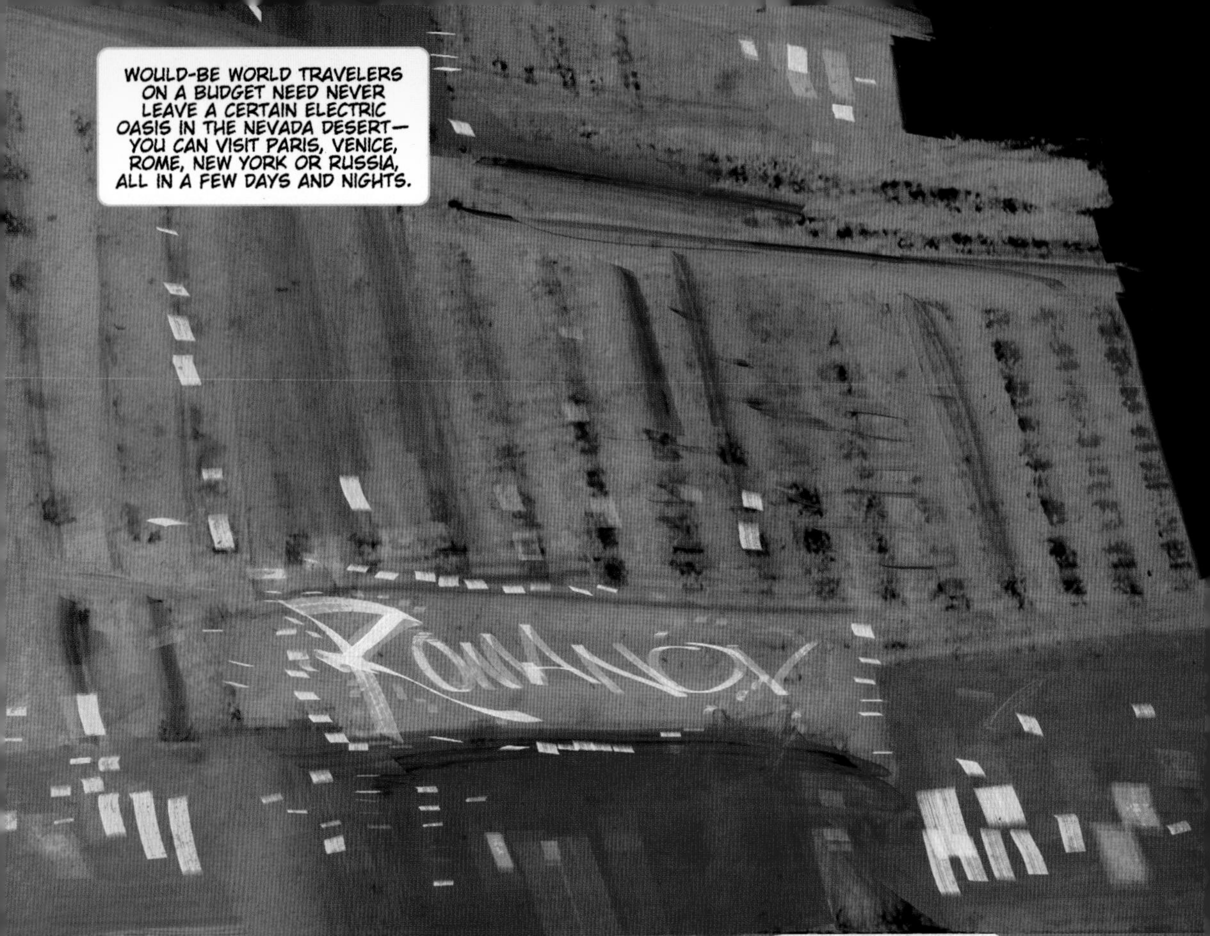
WOULD-BE WORLD TRAVELERS ON A BUDGET NEED NEVER LEAVE A CERTAIN ELECTRIC OASIS IN THE NEVADA DESERT— YOU CAN VISIT PARIS, VENICE, ROME, NEW YORK OR RUSSIA, ALL IN A FEW DAYS AND NIGHTS.

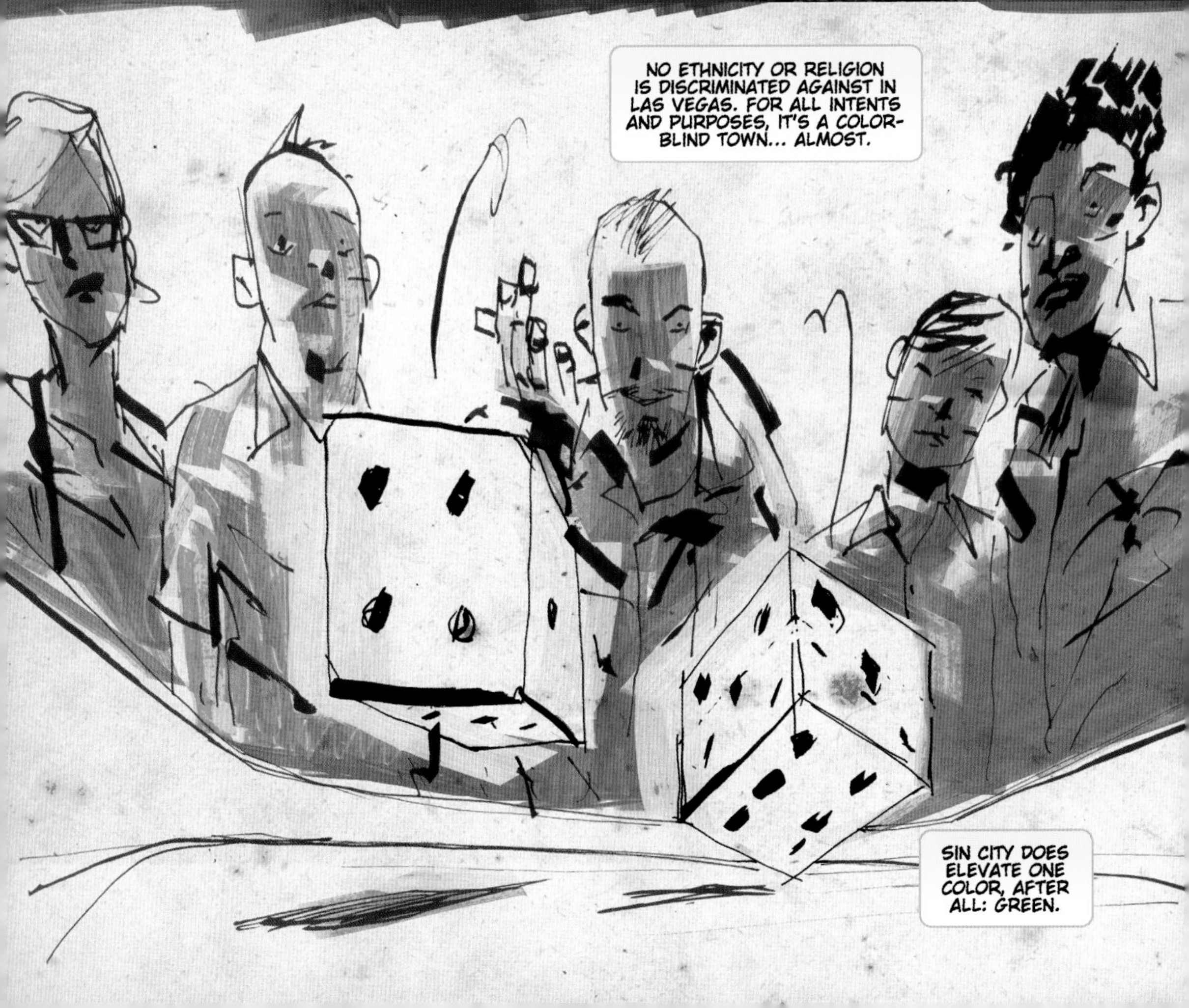
NO ETHNICITY OR RELIGION IS DISCRIMINATED AGAINST IN LAS VEGAS. FOR ALL INTENTS AND PURPOSES, IT'S A COLOR-BLIND TOWN... ALMOST.
SIN CITY DOES ELEVATE ONE COLOR, AFTER ALL: GREEN.

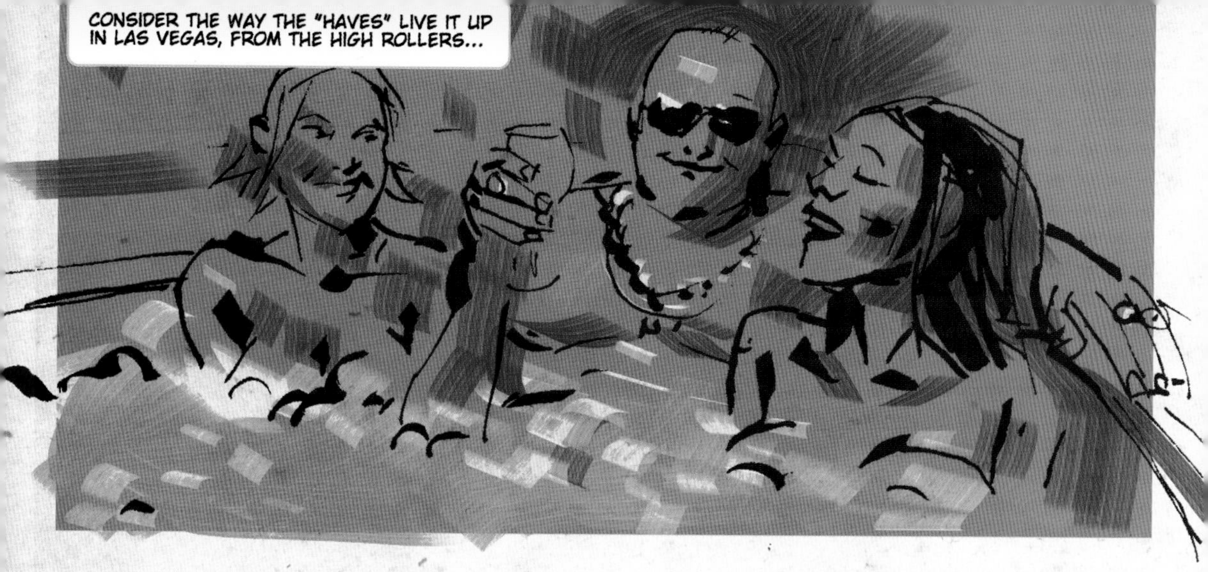
CONSIDER THE WAY THE "HAVES" LIVE IT UP IN LAS VEGAS, FROM THE HIGH ROLLERS...

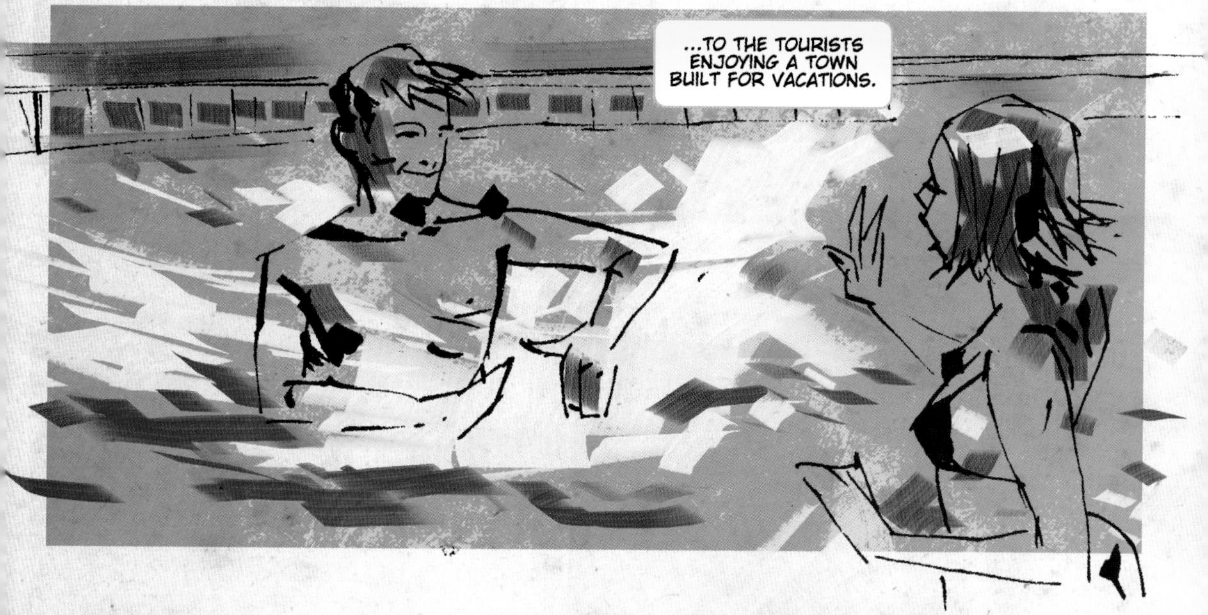
...TO THE TOURISTS ENJOYING A TOWN BUILT FOR VACATIONS.

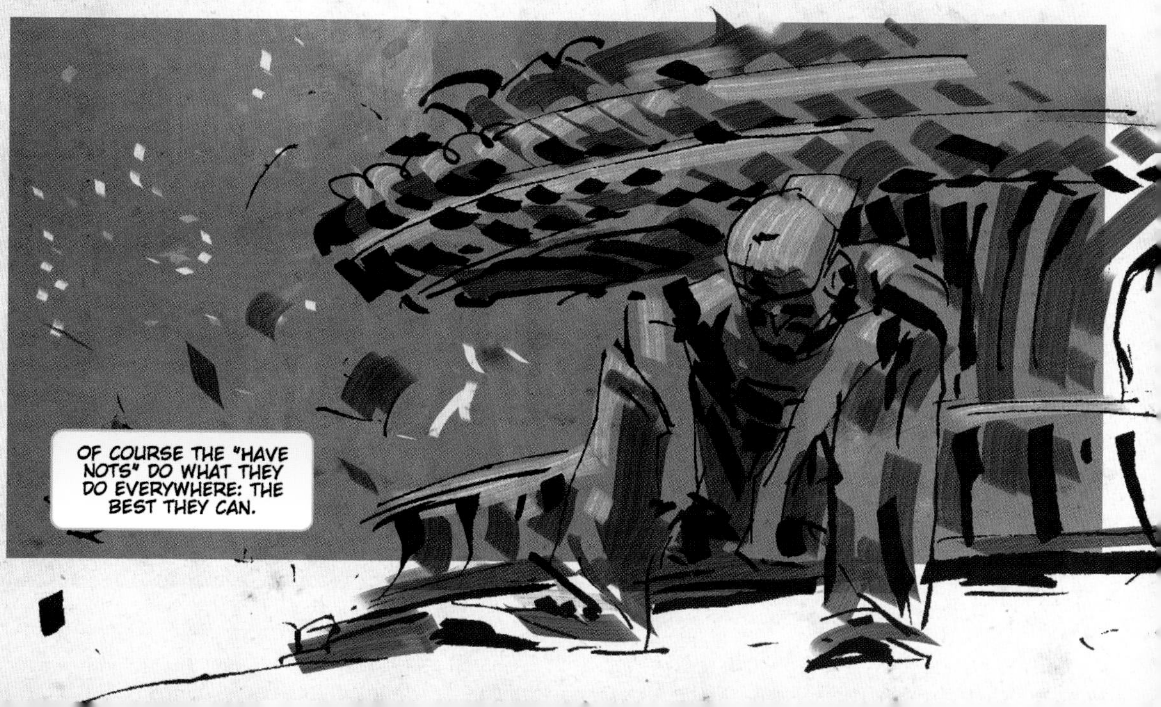
OF COURSE THE "HAVE NOTS" DO WHAT THEY DO EVERYWHERE: THE BEST THEY CAN.

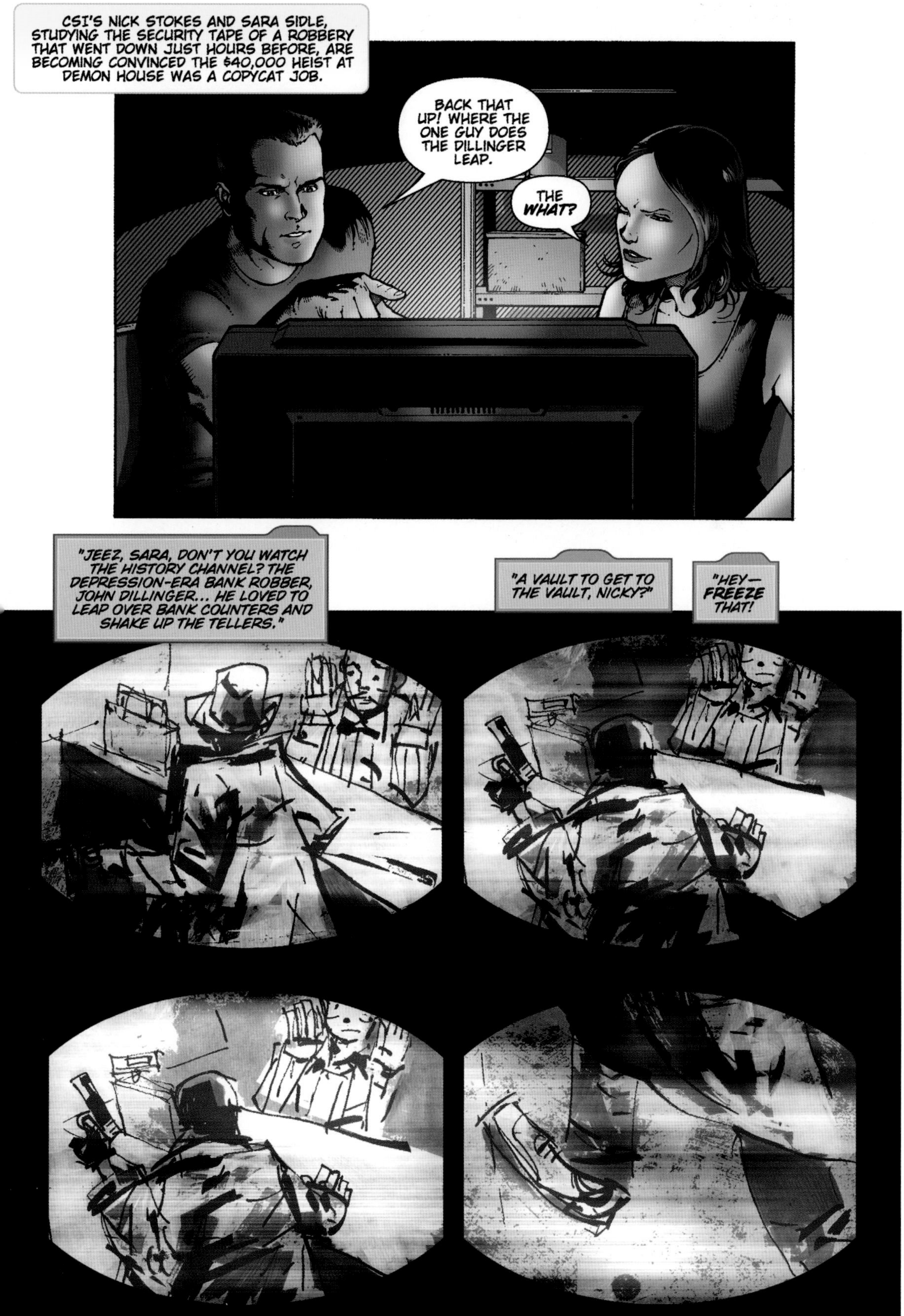

CSI'S NICK STOKES AND SARA SIDLE, STUDYING THE SECURITY TAPE OF A ROBBERY THAT WENT DOWN JUST HOURS BEFORE, ARE BECOMING CONVINCED THE $40,000 HEIST AT DEMON HOUSE WAS A COPYCAT JOB.
BACK THAT UP! WHERE THE ONE GUY DOES THE DILLINGER LEAP.
THE *WHAT?*
"JEEZ, SARA, DON'T YOU WATCH THE HISTORY CHANNEL? THE DEPRESSION-ERA BANK ROBBER, JOHN DILLINGER... HE LOVED TO LEAP OVER BANK COUNTERS AND SHAKE UP THE TELLERS."
"A VAULT TO GET TO THE VAULT, NICKY?"
"HEY— **FREEZE** THAT!
"NOW, **ZOOM** IN, SARA."
"I'M WITH YOU, NICK— RUNNING SHOES!"

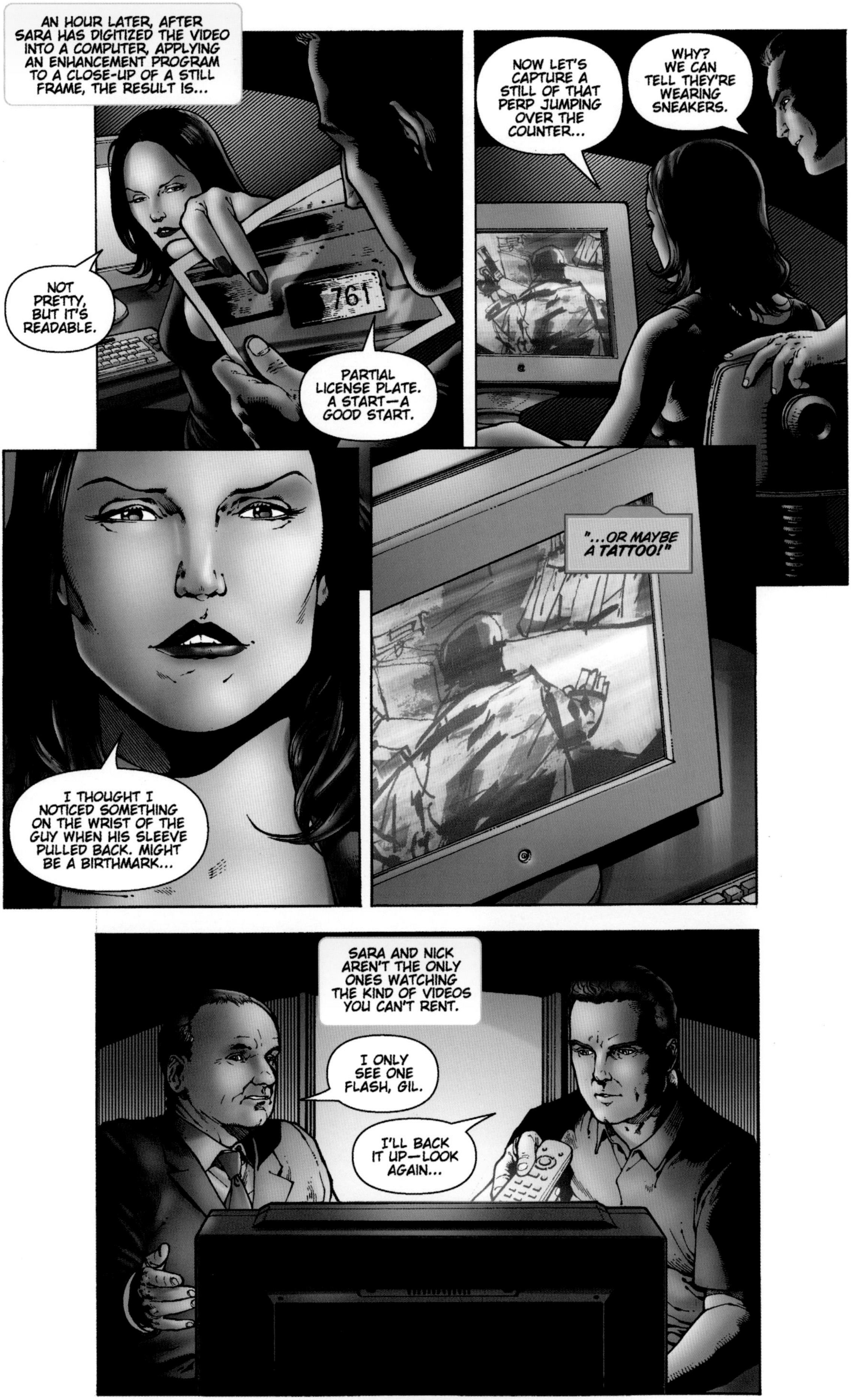
AN HOUR LATER, AFTER SARA HAS DIGITIZED THE VIDEO INTO A COMPUTER, APPLYING AN ENHANCEMENT PROGRAM TO A CLOSE-UP OF A STILL FRAME, THE RESULT IS...
NOT PRETTY, BUT IT'S READABLE.
761
PARTIAL LICENSE PLATE. A START—A GOOD START.
NOW LET'S CAPTURE A STILL OF THAT PERP JUMPING OVER THE COUNTER...
WHY? WE CAN TELL THEY'RE WEARING SNEAKERS.
I THOUGHT I NOTICED SOMETHING ON THE WRIST OF THE GUY WHEN HIS SLEEVE PULLED BACK. MIGHT BE A BIRTHMARK...
"...OR MAYBE A TATTOO!"
SARA AND NICK AREN'T THE ONLY ONES WATCHING THE KIND OF VIDEOS YOU CAN'T RENT.
I ONLY SEE ONE FLASH, GIL.
I'LL BACK IT UP—LOOK AGAIN...

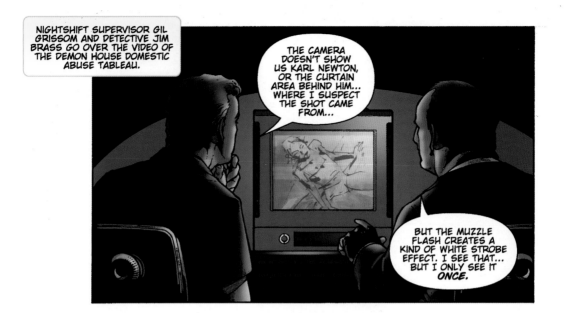

NIGHTSHIFT SUPERVISOR GIL GRISSOM AND DETECTIVE JIM BRASS GO OVER THE VIDEO OF THE DEMON HOUSE DOMESTIC ABUSE TABLEAU.

THE CAMERA DOESN'T SHOW US KARL NEWTON, OR THE CURTAIN AREA BEHIND HIM... WHERE I SUSPECT THE SHOT CAME FROM...

BUT THE MUZZLE FLASH CREATES A KIND OF WHITE STROBE EFFECT. I SEE THAT... BUT I ONLY SEE IT ONCE.

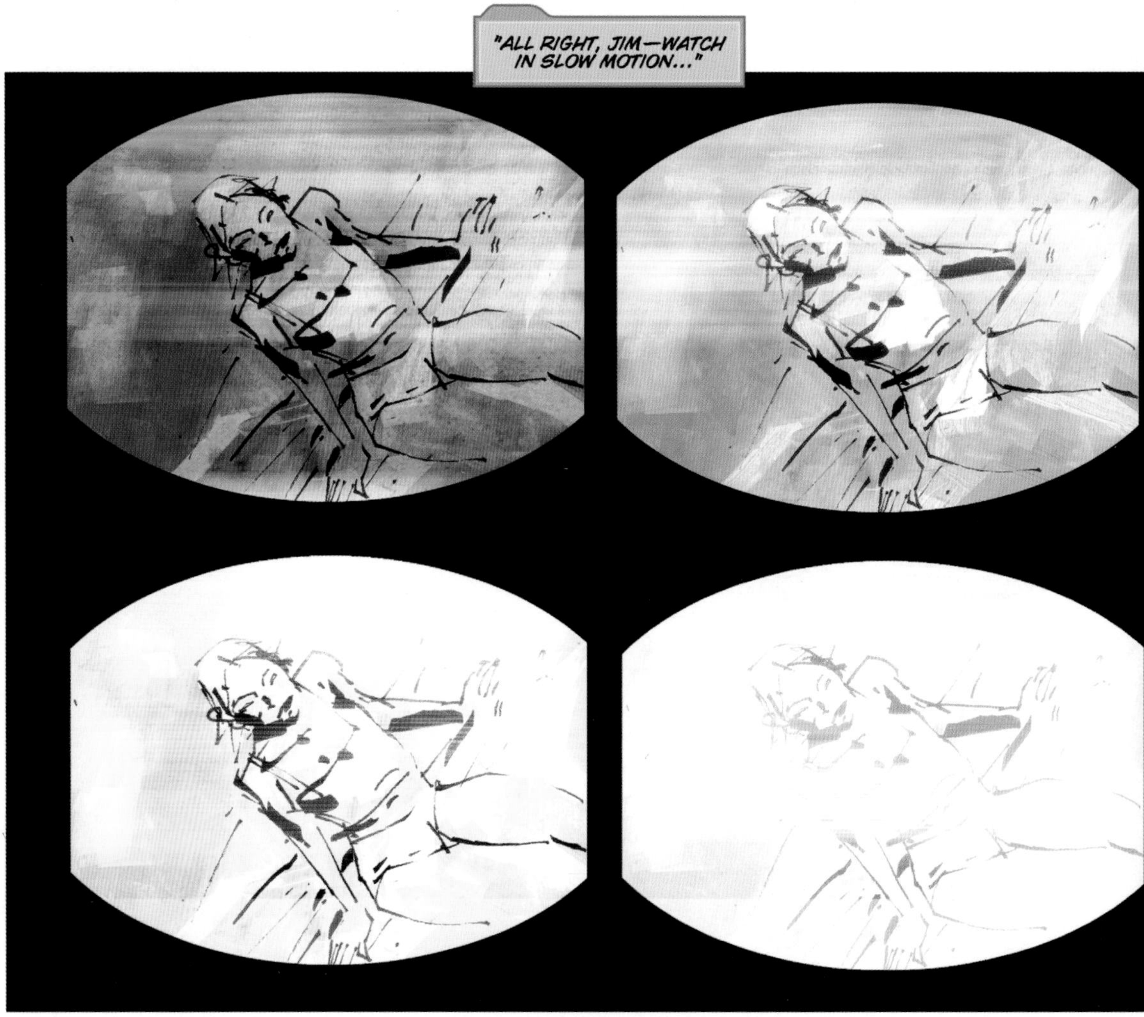

"ALL RIGHT, JIM—WATCH IN SLOW MOTION..."

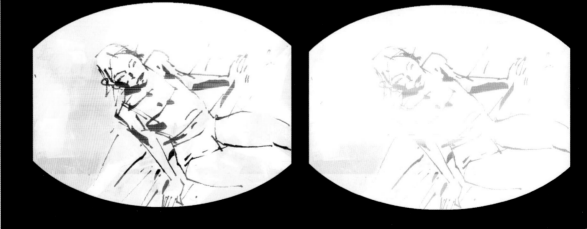

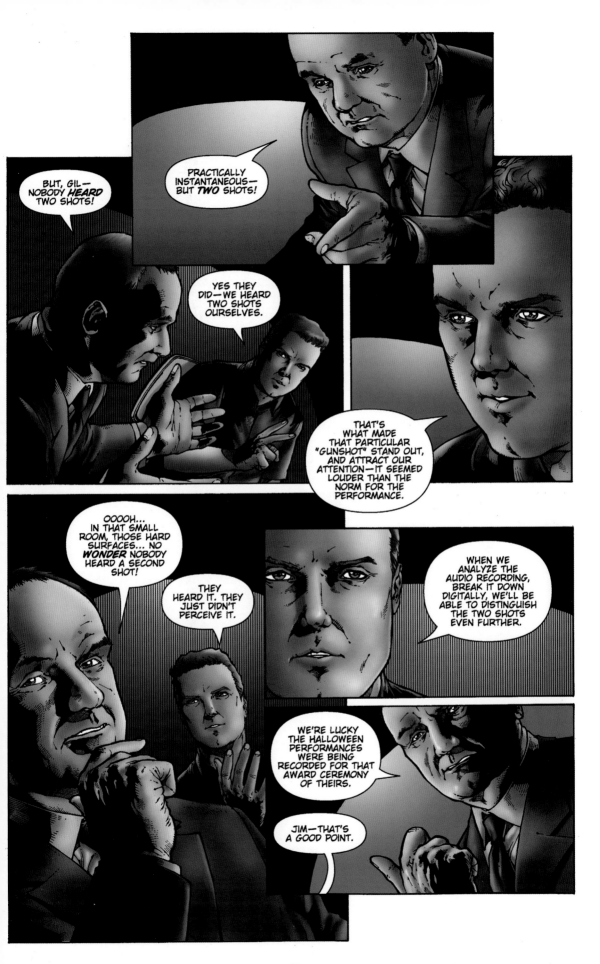

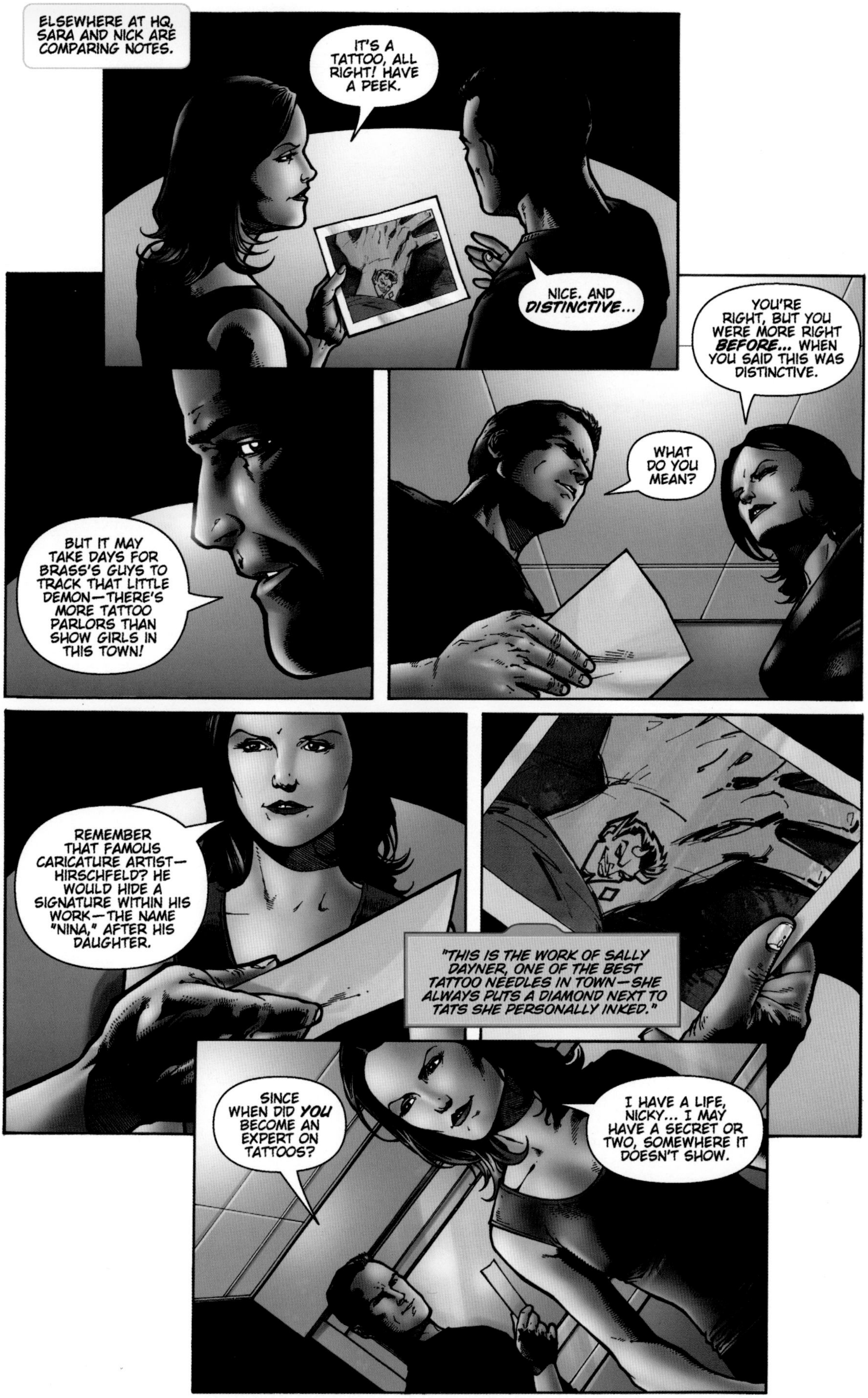
ELSEWHERE AT HQ, SARA AND NICK ARE COMPARING NOTES.
IT'S A TATTOO, ALL RIGHT! HAVE A PEEK.
NICE. AND *DISTINCTIVE*...
BUT IT MAY TAKE DAYS FOR BRASS'S GUYS TO TRACK THAT LITTLE DEMON—THERE'S MORE TATTOO PARLORS THAN SHOW GIRLS IN THIS TOWN!
YOU'RE RIGHT, BUT YOU WERE MORE RIGHT *BEFORE*... WHEN YOU SAID THIS WAS DISTINCTIVE.
WHAT DO YOU MEAN?
REMEMBER THAT FAMOUS CARICATURE ARTIST—HIRSCHFELD? HE WOULD HIDE A SIGNATURE WITHIN HIS WORK—THE NAME "NINA," AFTER HIS DAUGHTER.
"THIS IS THE WORK OF SALLY DAYNER, ONE OF THE BEST TATTOO NEEDLES IN TOWN—SHE ALWAYS PUTS A DIAMOND NEXT TO TATS SHE PERSONALLY INKED."
SINCE WHEN DID *YOU* BECOME AN EXPERT ON TATTOOS?
I HAVE A LIFE, NICKY... I MAY HAVE A SECRET OR TWO, SOMEWHERE IT DOESN'T SHOW.

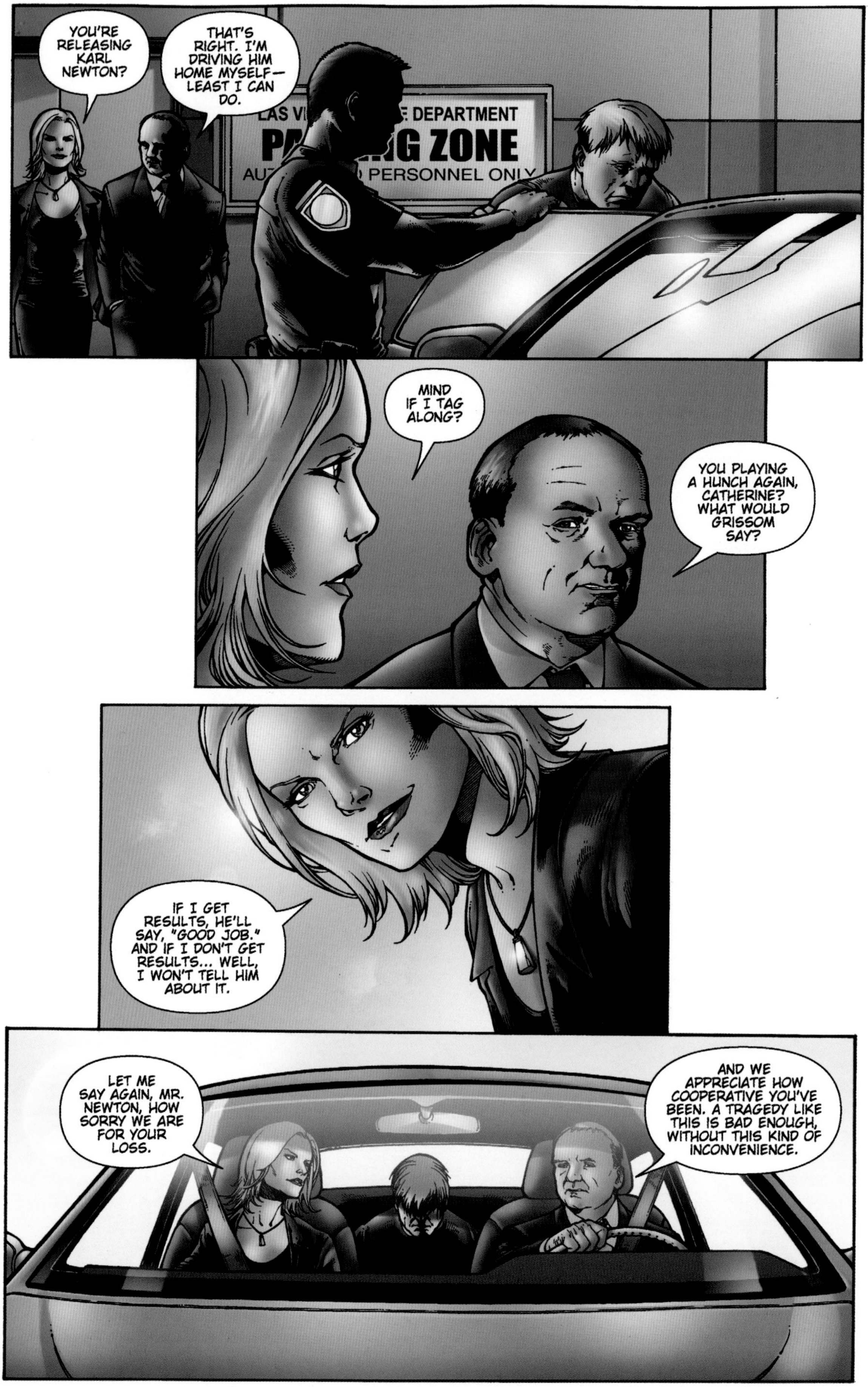
YOU'RE RELEASING KARL NEWTON?
THAT'S RIGHT. I'M DRIVING HIM HOME MYSELF— LEAST I CAN DO.
DEPARTMENT
ZONE
PERSONNEL ONLY
MIND IF I TAG ALONG?
YOU PLAYING A HUNCH AGAIN, CATHERINE? WHAT WOULD GRISSOM SAY?
IF I GET RESULTS, HE'LL SAY, "GOOD JOB." AND IF I DON'T GET RESULTS... WELL, I WON'T TELL HIM ABOUT IT.
LET ME SAY AGAIN, MR. NEWTON, HOW SORRY WE ARE FOR YOUR LOSS.
AND WE APPRECIATE HOW COOPERATIVE YOU'VE BEEN. A TRAGEDY LIKE THIS IS BAD ENOUGH, WITHOUT THIS KIND OF INCONVENIENCE.

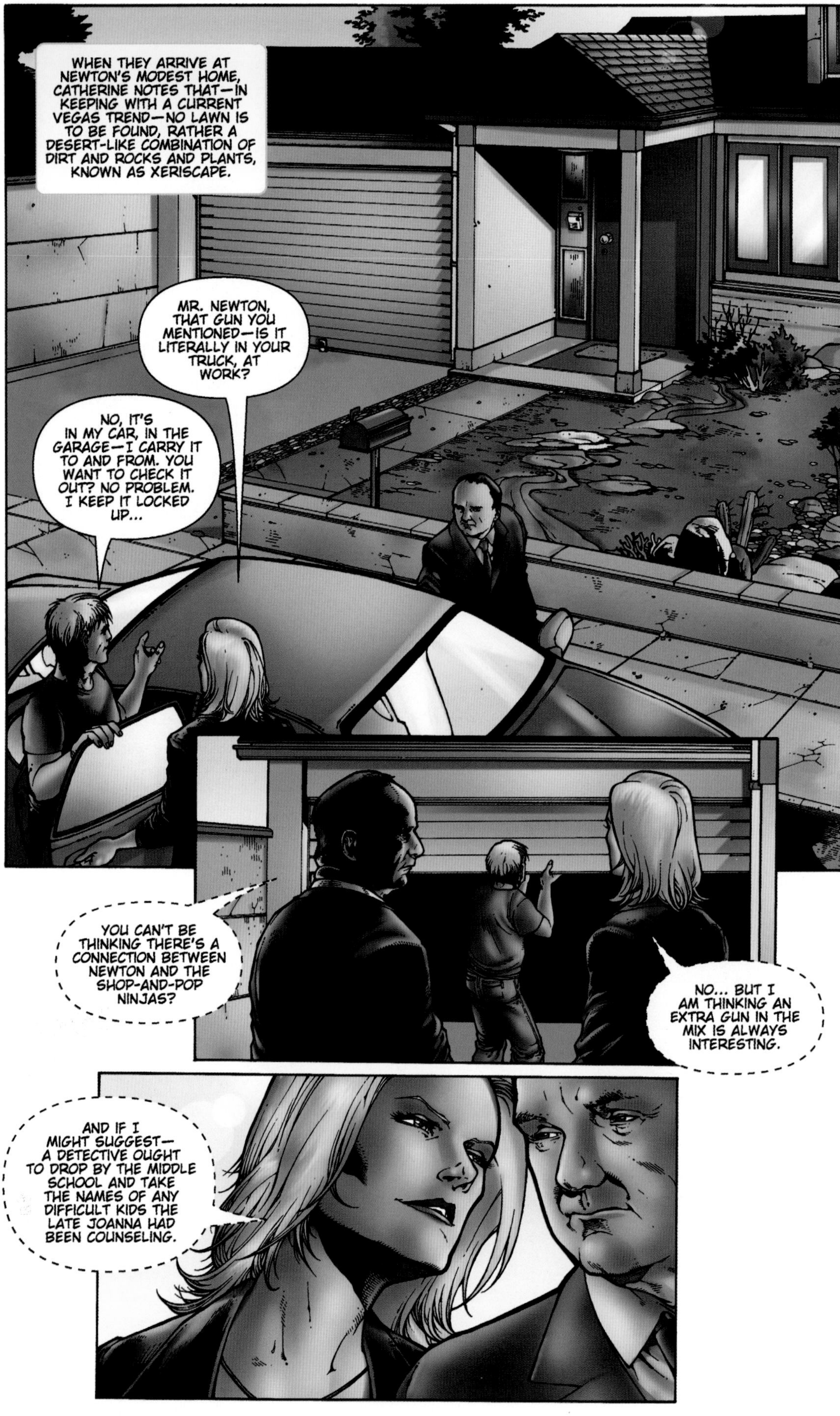
WHEN THEY ARRIVE AT NEWTON'S MODEST HOME, CATHERINE NOTES THAT—IN KEEPING WITH A CURRENT VEGAS TREND—NO LAWN IS TO BE FOUND, RATHER A DESERT-LIKE COMBINATION OF DIRT AND ROCKS AND PLANTS, KNOWN AS XERISCAPE.
MR. NEWTON, THAT GUN YOU MENTIONED—IS IT LITERALLY IN YOUR TRUCK, AT WORK?
NO, IT'S IN MY CAR, IN THE GARAGE—I CARRY IT TO AND FROM. YOU WANT TO CHECK IT OUT? NO PROBLEM. I KEEP IT LOCKED UP...
YOU CAN'T BE THINKING THERE'S A CONNECTION BETWEEN NEWTON AND THE SHOP-AND-POP NINJAS?
NO... BUT I AM THINKING AN EXTRA GUN IN THE MIX IS ALWAYS INTERESTING.
AND IF I MIGHT SUGGEST—A DETECTIVE OUGHT TO DROP BY THE MIDDLE SCHOOL AND TAKE THE NAMES OF ANY DIFFICULT KIDS THE LATE JOANNA HAD BEEN COUNSELING.

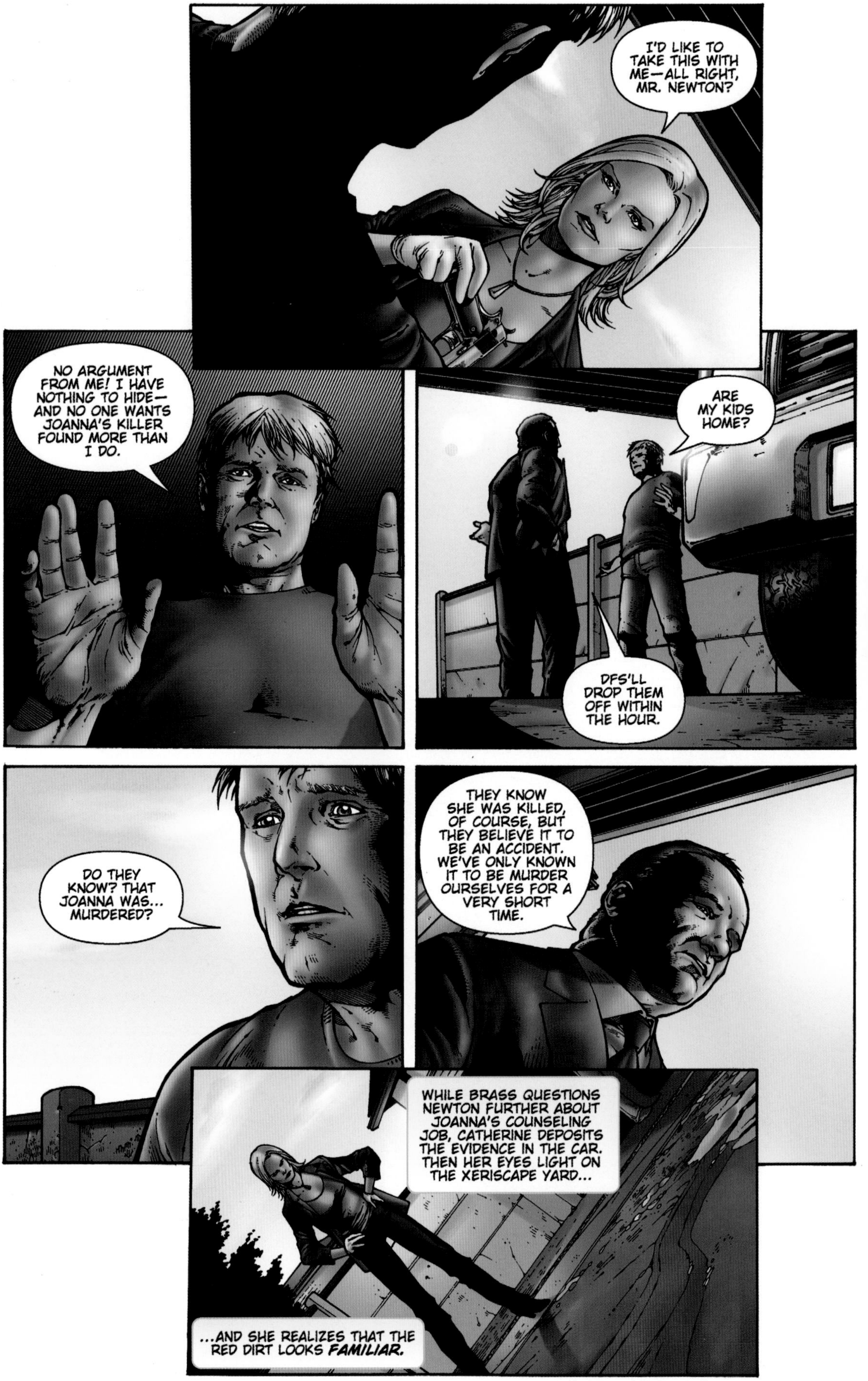
I'D LIKE TO TAKE THIS WITH ME—ALL RIGHT, MR. NEWTON?
NO ARGUMENT FROM ME! I HAVE NOTHING TO HIDE—AND NO ONE WANTS JOANNA'S KILLER FOUND MORE THAN I DO.
ARE MY KIDS HOME?
DFS'LL DROP THEM OFF WITHIN THE HOUR.
DO THEY KNOW? THAT JOANNA WAS... MURDERED?
THEY KNOW SHE WAS KILLED, OF COURSE, BUT THEY BELIEVE IT TO BE AN ACCIDENT. WE'VE ONLY KNOWN IT TO BE MURDER OURSELVES FOR A VERY SHORT TIME.
WHILE BRASS QUESTIONS NEWTON FURTHER ABOUT JOANNA'S COUNSELING JOB, CATHERINE DEPOSITS THE EVIDENCE IN THE CAR. THEN HER EYES LIGHT ON THE XERISCAPE YARD...
...AND SHE REALIZES THAT THE RED DIRT LOOKS FAMILIAR.

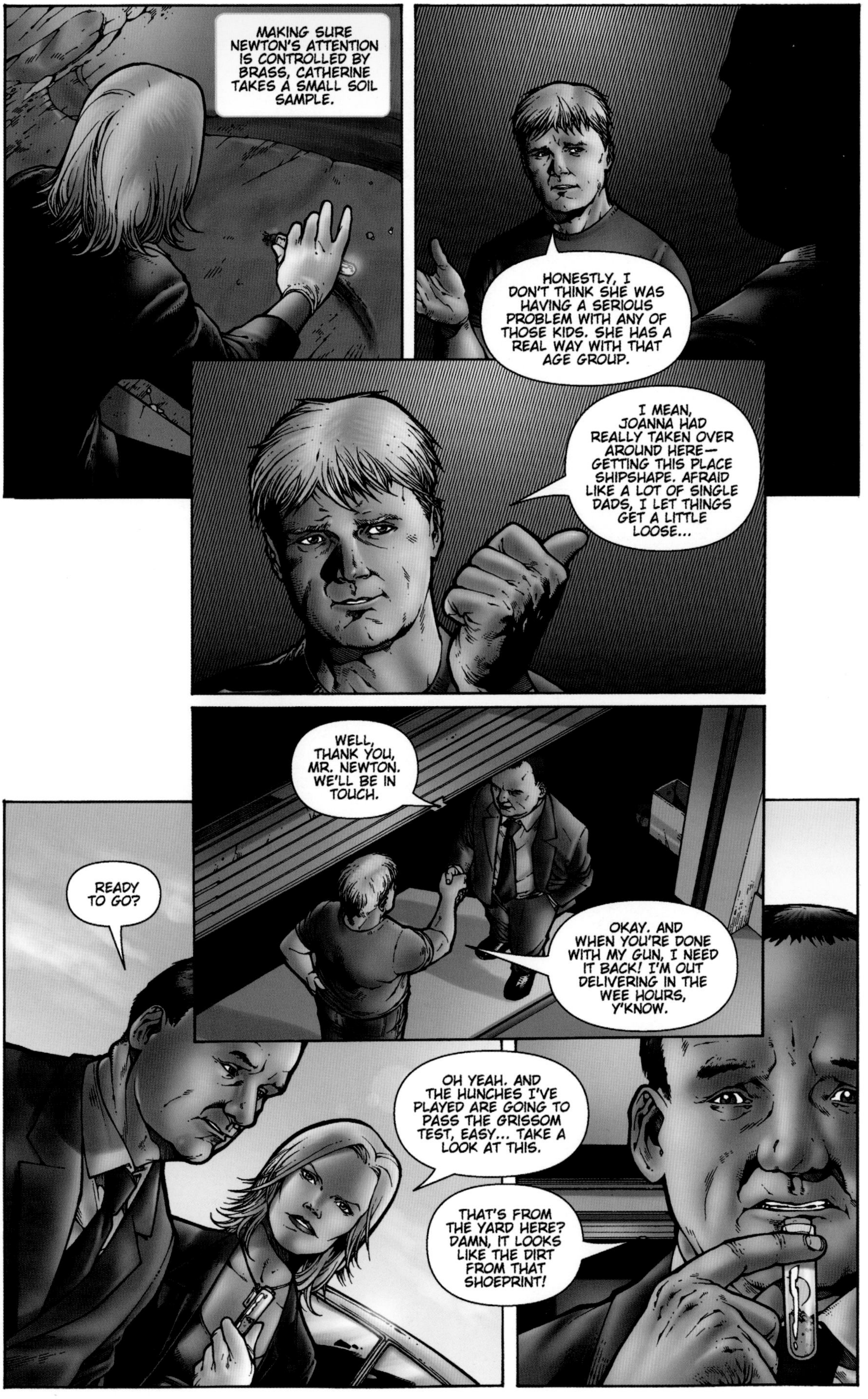
MAKING SURE NEWTON'S ATTENTION IS CONTROLLED BY BRASS, CATHERINE TAKES A SMALL SOIL SAMPLE.
HONESTLY, I DON'T THINK SHE WAS HAVING A SERIOUS PROBLEM WITH ANY OF THOSE KIDS. SHE HAS A REAL WAY WITH THAT AGE GROUP.
I MEAN, JOANNA HAD REALLY TAKEN OVER AROUND HERE—GETTING THIS PLACE SHIPSHAPE. AFRAID LIKE A LOT OF SINGLE DADS, I LET THINGS GET A LITTLE LOOSE...
WELL, THANK YOU, MR. NEWTON. WE'LL BE IN TOUCH.
OKAY. AND WHEN YOU'RE DONE WITH MY GUN, I NEED IT BACK! I'M OUT DELIVERING IN THE WEE HOURS, Y'KNOW.
READY TO GO?
OH YEAH. AND THE HUNCHES I'VE PLAYED ARE GOING TO PASS THE GRISSOM TEST, EASY... TAKE A LOOK AT THIS.
THAT'S FROM THE YARD HERE? DAMN, IT LOOKS LIKE THE DIRT FROM THAT SHOEPRINT!

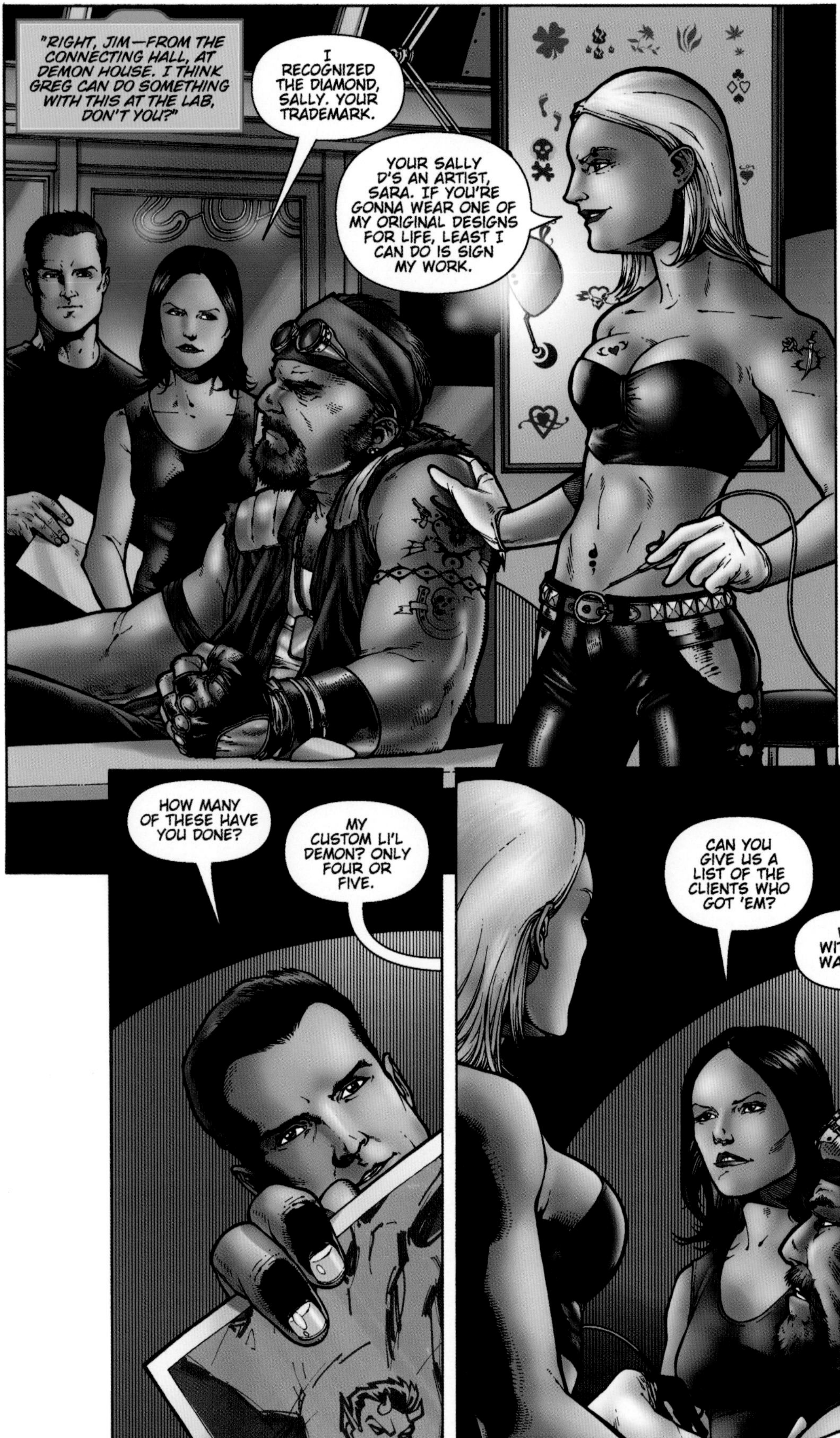
"RIGHT, JIM—FROM THE CONNECTING HALL, AT DEMON HOUSE. I THINK GREG CAN DO SOMETHING WITH THIS AT THE LAB, DON'T YOU?"
I RECOGNIZED THE DIAMOND, SALLY. YOUR TRADEMARK.
YOUR SALLY D'S AN ARTIST, SARA. IF YOU'RE GONNA WEAR ONE OF MY ORIGINAL DESIGNS FOR LIFE, LEAST I CAN DO IS SIGN MY WORK.
HOW MANY OF THESE HAVE YOU DONE?
MY CUSTOM LI'L DEMON? ONLY FOUR OR FIVE.
CAN YOU GIVE US A LIST OF THE CLIENTS WHO GOT 'EM?
WHAT, WITHOUT A WARRANT?

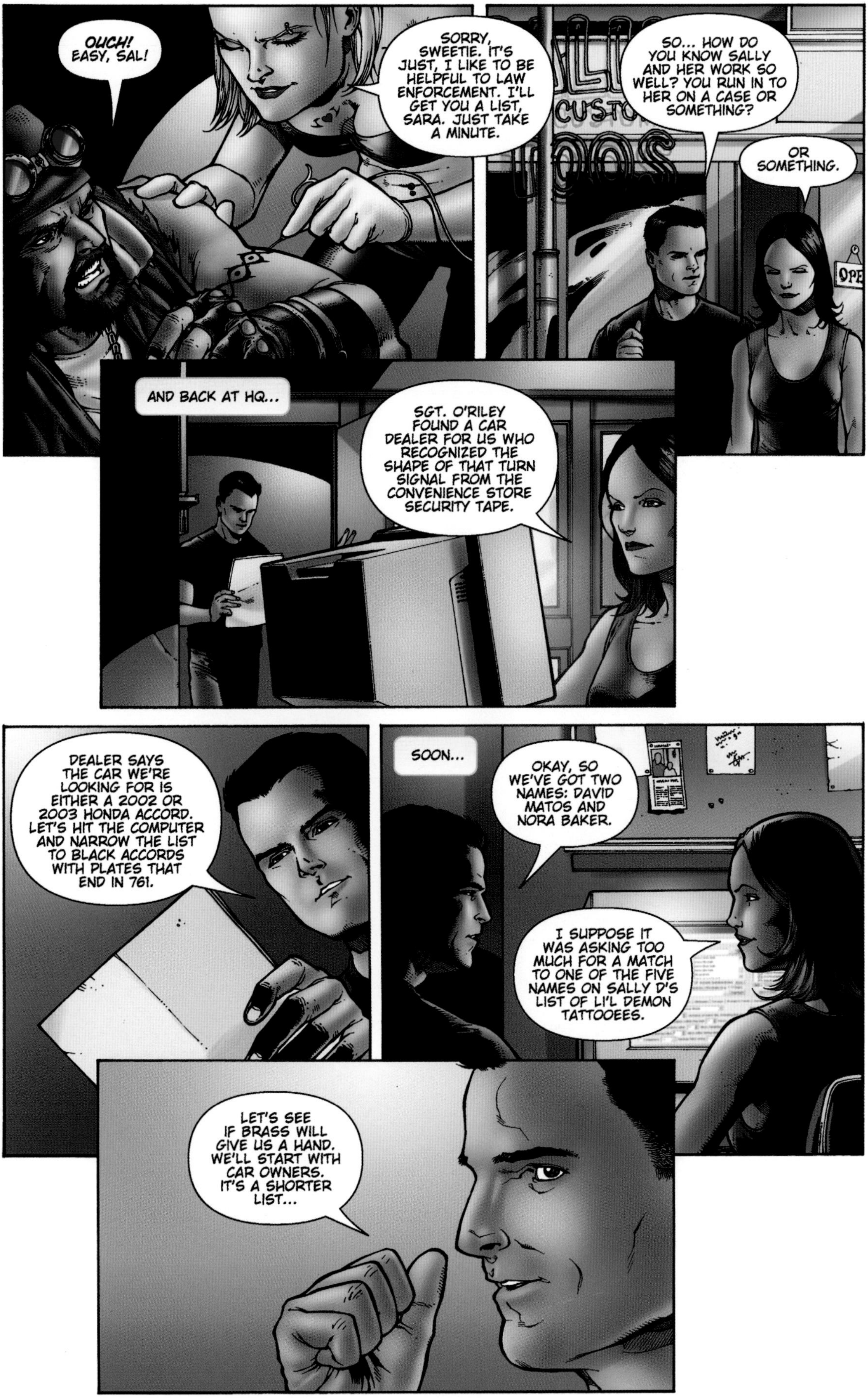

OUCH! EASY, SAL!
SORRY, SWEETIE. IT'S JUST, I LIKE TO BE HELPFUL TO LAW ENFORCEMENT. I'LL GET YOU A LIST, SARA. JUST TAKE A MINUTE.
SO... HOW DO YOU KNOW SALLY AND HER WORK SO WELL? YOU RUN IN TO HER ON A CASE OR SOMETHING?
OR SOMETHING.
AND BACK AT HQ...
SGT. O'RILEY FOUND A CAR DEALER FOR US WHO RECOGNIZED THE SHAPE OF THAT TURN SIGNAL FROM THE CONVENIENCE STORE SECURITY TAPE.
DEALER SAYS THE CAR WE'RE LOOKING FOR IS EITHER A 2002 OR 2003 HONDA ACCORD. LET'S HIT THE COMPUTER AND NARROW THE LIST TO BLACK ACCORDS WITH PLATES THAT END IN 761.
SOON...
OKAY, SO WE'VE GOT TWO NAMES: DAVID MATOS AND NORA BAKER.
I SUPPOSE IT WAS ASKING TOO MUCH FOR A MATCH TO ONE OF THE FIVE NAMES ON SALLY D'S LIST OF LI'L DEMON TATTOOEES.
LET'S SEE IF BRASS WILL GIVE US A HAND. WE'LL START WITH CAR OWNERS. IT'S A SHORTER LIST...

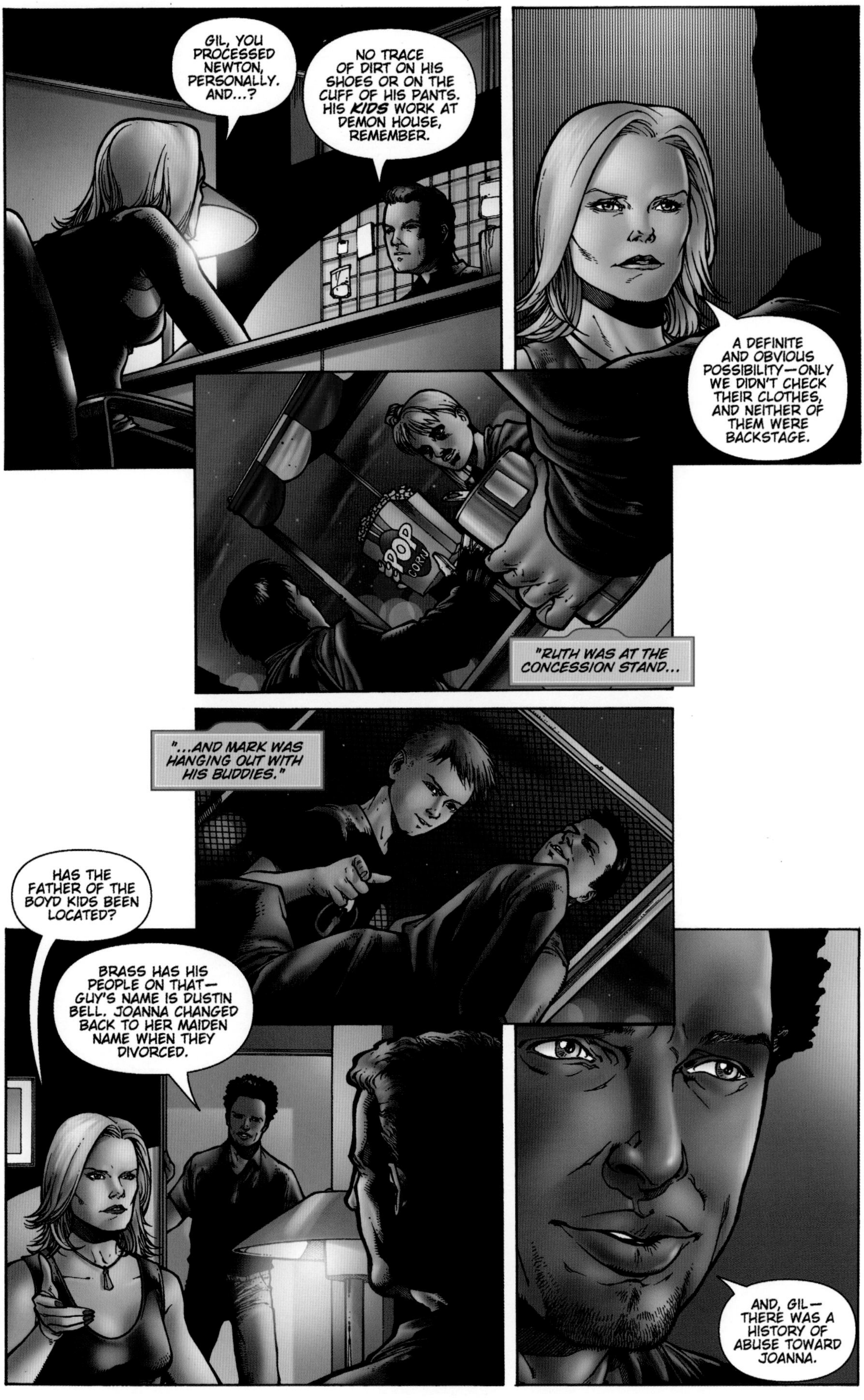

GIL, YOU PROCESSED NEWTON, PERSONALLY. AND...?
NO TRACE OF DIRT ON HIS SHOES OR ON THE CUFF OF HIS PANTS. HIS KIDS WORK AT DEMON HOUSE, REMEMBER.
A DEFINITE AND OBVIOUS POSSIBILITY—ONLY WE DIDN'T CHECK THEIR CLOTHES, AND NEITHER OF THEM WERE BACKSTAGE.
"RUTH WAS AT THE CONCESSION STAND...
"...AND MARK WAS HANGING OUT WITH HIS BUDDIES."
HAS THE FATHER OF THE BOYD KIDS BEEN LOCATED?
BRASS HAS HIS PEOPLE ON THAT—GUY'S NAME IS DUSTIN BELL. JOANNA CHANGED BACK TO HER MAIDEN NAME WHEN THEY DIVORCED.
AND, GIL—THERE WAS A HISTORY OF ABUSE TOWARD JOANNA.

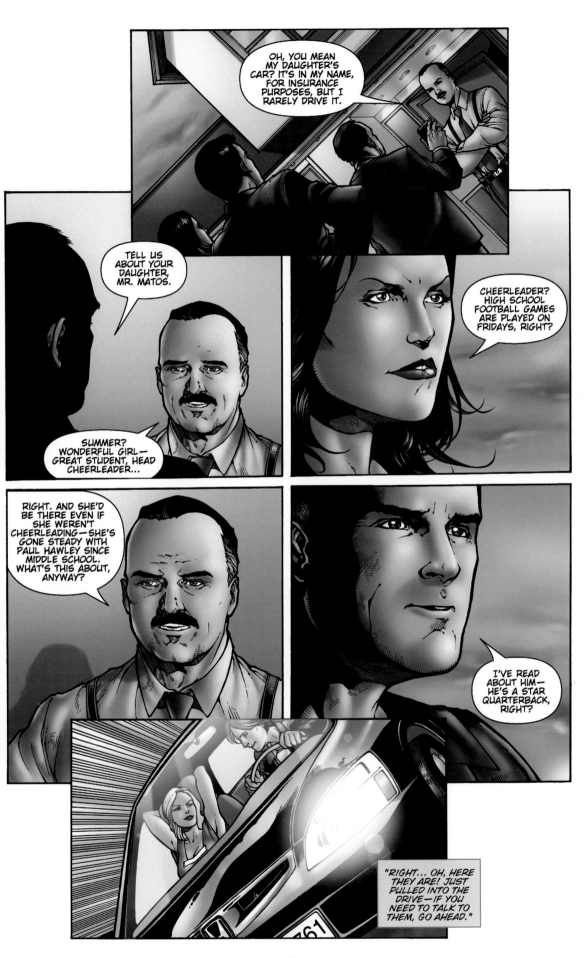

Chapter 5
"Just Say No"

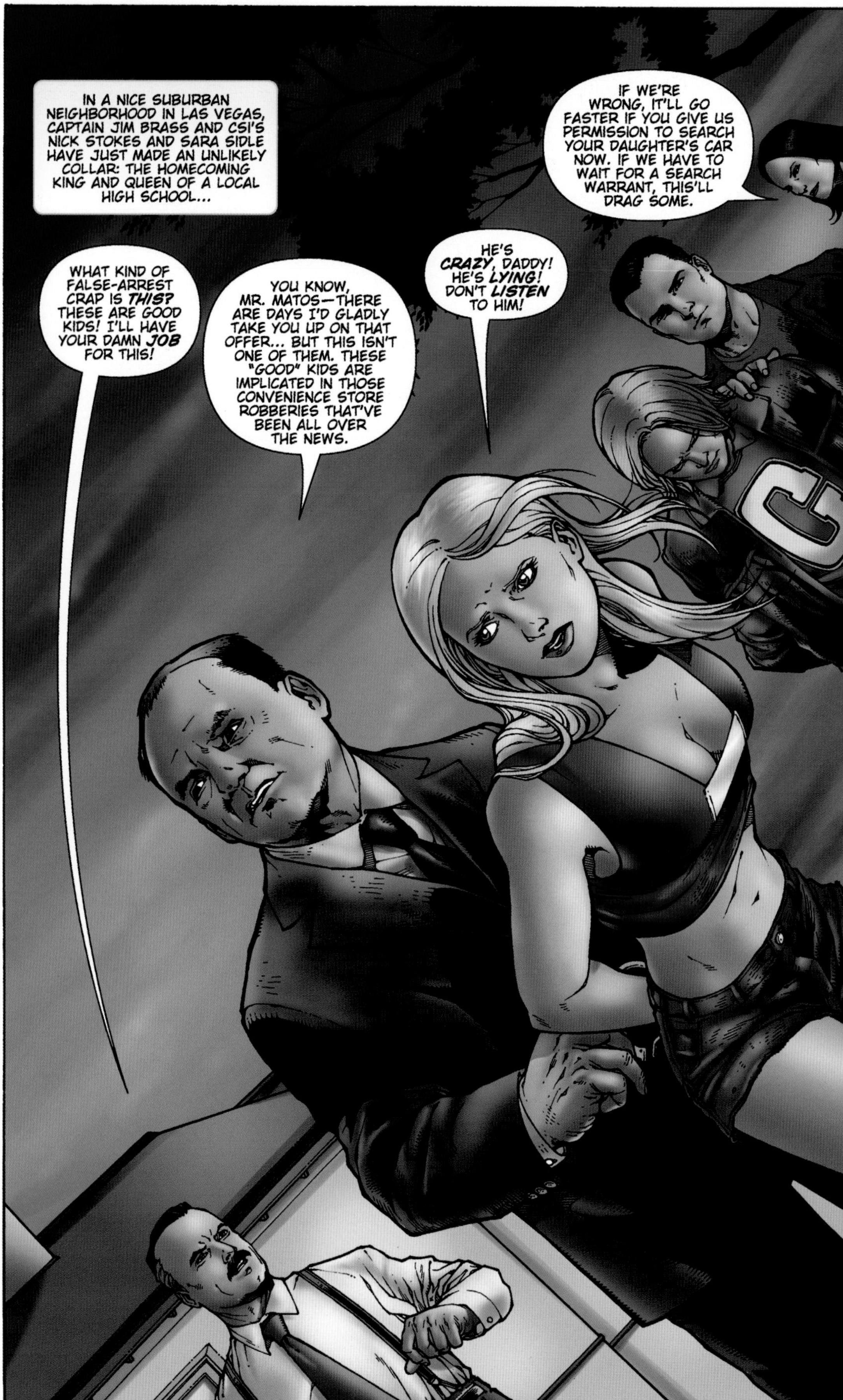
IN A NICE SUBURBAN NEIGHBORHOOD IN LAS VEGAS, CAPTAIN JIM BRASS AND CSI'S NICK STOKES AND SARA SIDLE HAVE JUST MADE AN UNLIKELY COLLAR: THE HOMECOMING KING AND QUEEN OF A LOCAL HIGH SCHOOL...
IF WE'RE WRONG, IT'LL GO FASTER IF YOU GIVE US PERMISSION TO SEARCH YOUR DAUGHTER'S CAR NOW. IF WE HAVE TO WAIT FOR A SEARCH WARRANT, THIS'LL DRAG SOME.
WHAT KIND OF FALSE-ARREST CRAP IS *THIS?* THESE ARE GOOD KIDS! I'LL HAVE YOUR DAMN *JOB* FOR THIS!
YOU KNOW, MR. MATOS—THERE ARE DAYS I'D GLADLY TAKE YOU UP ON THAT OFFER... BUT THIS ISN'T ONE OF THEM. THESE "GOOD" KIDS ARE IMPLICATED IN THOSE CONVENIENCE STORE ROBBERIES THAT'VE BEEN ALL OVER THE NEWS.
HE'S *CRAZY*, DADDY! HE'S *LYING!* DON'T *LISTEN* TO HIM!

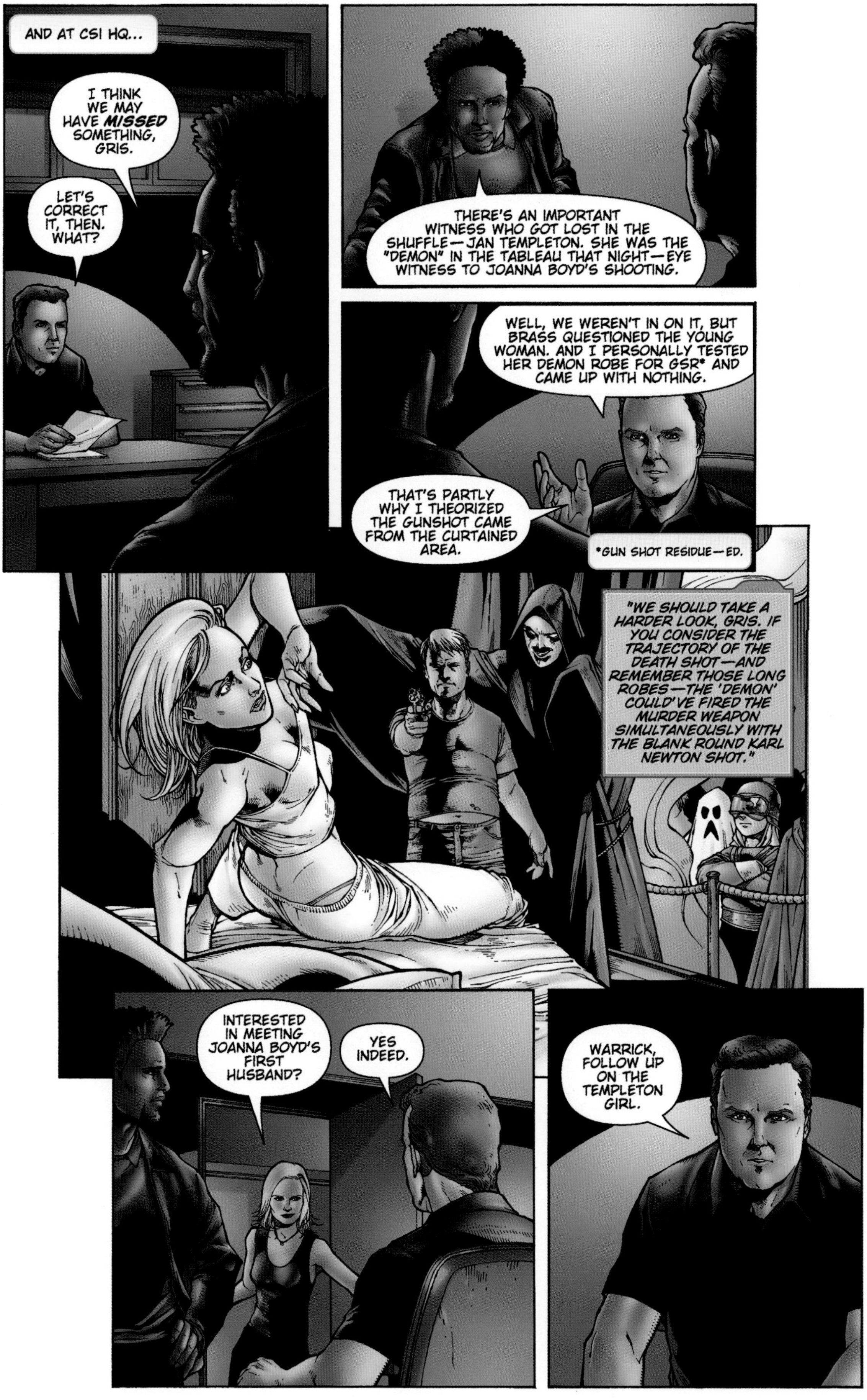
AND AT CSI HQ...
I THINK WE MAY HAVE MISSED SOMETHING, GRIS.
LET'S CORRECT IT, THEN. WHAT?
THERE'S AN IMPORTANT WITNESS WHO GOT LOST IN THE SHUFFLE—JAN TEMPLETON. SHE WAS THE "DEMON" IN THE TABLEAU THAT NIGHT—EYE WITNESS TO JOANNA BOYD'S SHOOTING.
WELL, WE WEREN'T IN ON IT, BUT BRASS QUESTIONED THE YOUNG WOMAN. AND I PERSONALLY TESTED HER DEMON ROBE FOR GSR* AND CAME UP WITH NOTHING.
THAT'S PARTLY WHY I THEORIZED THE GUNSHOT CAME FROM THE CURTAINED AREA.
*GUN SHOT RESIDUE—ED.
"WE SHOULD TAKE A HARDER LOOK, GRIS. IF YOU CONSIDER THE TRAJECTORY OF THE DEATH SHOT—AND REMEMBER THOSE LONG ROBES—THE 'DEMON' COULD'VE FIRED THE MURDER WEAPON SIMULTANEOUSLY WITH THE BLANK ROUND KARL NEWTON SHOT."
INTERESTED IN MEETING JOANNA BOYD'S FIRST HUSBAND?
YES INDEED.
WARRICK, FOLLOW UP ON THE TEMPLETON GIRL.

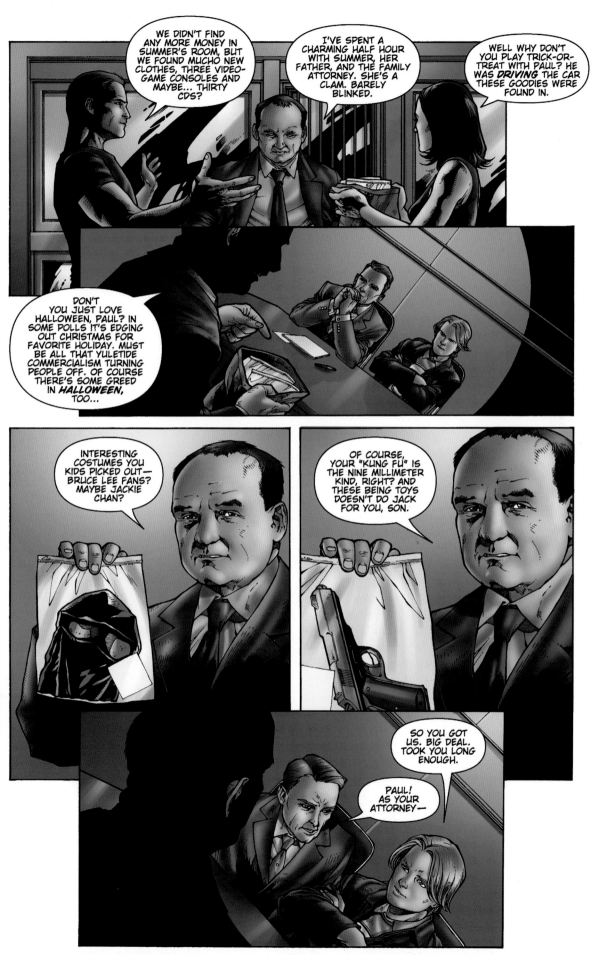

WE DIDN'T FIND ANY MORE MONEY IN SUMMER'S ROOM, BUT WE FOUND MUCHO NEW CLOTHES, THREE VIDEO-GAME CONSOLES AND MAYBE... THIRTY CDS?

I'VE SPENT A CHARMING HALF HOUR WITH SUMMER, HER FATHER, AND THE FAMILY ATTORNEY. SHE'S A CLAM. BARELY BLINKED.

WELL WHY DON'T YOU PLAY TRICK-OR-TREAT WITH PAUL? HE WAS *DRIVING* THE CAR THESE GOODIES WERE FOUND IN.

DON'T YOU JUST LOVE HALLOWEEN, PAUL? IN SOME POLLS IT'S EDGING OUT CHRISTMAS FOR FAVORITE HOLIDAY. MUST BE ALL THAT YULETIDE COMMERCIALISM TURNING PEOPLE OFF. OF COURSE THERE'S SOME GREED IN *HALLOWEEN*, TOO...

INTERESTING COSTUMES YOU KIDS PICKED OUT—BRUCE LEE FANS? MAYBE JACKIE CHAN?

OF COURSE, YOUR "KUNG FU" IS THE NINE MILLIMETER KIND, RIGHT? AND THESE BEING TOYS DOESN'T DO JACK FOR YOU, SON.

SO YOU GOT US. BIG DEAL. TOOK YOU LONG ENOUGH.

PAUL! AS YOUR ATTORNEY—

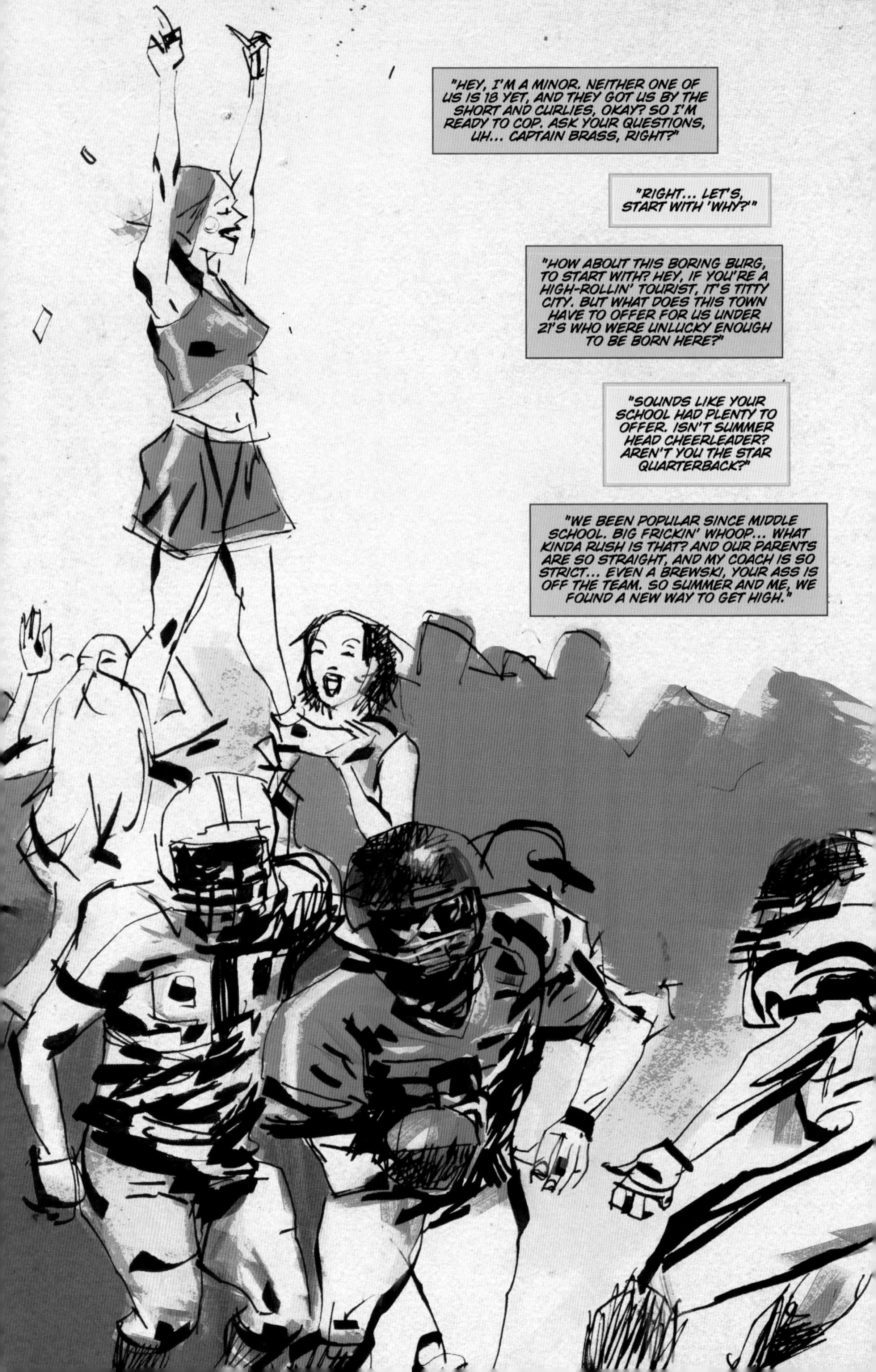
"HEY, I'M A MINOR. NEITHER ONE OF US IS 18 YET, AND THEY GOT US BY THE SHORT AND CURLIES, OKAY? SO I'M READY TO COP. ASK YOUR QUESTIONS, UH... CAPTAIN BRASS, RIGHT?"
"RIGHT... LET'S, START WITH 'WHY?'"
"HOW ABOUT THIS BORING BURG, TO START WITH? HEY, IF YOU'RE A HIGH-ROLLIN' TOURIST, IT'S TITTY CITY. BUT WHAT DOES THIS TOWN HAVE TO OFFER FOR US UNDER 21'S WHO WERE UNLUCKY ENOUGH TO BE BORN HERE?"
"SOUNDS LIKE YOUR SCHOOL HAD PLENTY TO OFFER. ISN'T SUMMER HEAD CHEERLEADER? AREN'T YOU THE STAR QUARTERBACK?"
"WE BEEN POPULAR SINCE MIDDLE SCHOOL. BIG FRICKIN' WHOOP... WHAT KINDA RUSH IS THAT? AND OUR PARENTS ARE SO STRAIGHT, AND MY COACH IS SO STRICT... EVEN A BREWSKI, YOUR ASS IS OFF THE TEAM. SO SUMMER AND ME, WE FOUND A NEW WAY TO GET HIGH."

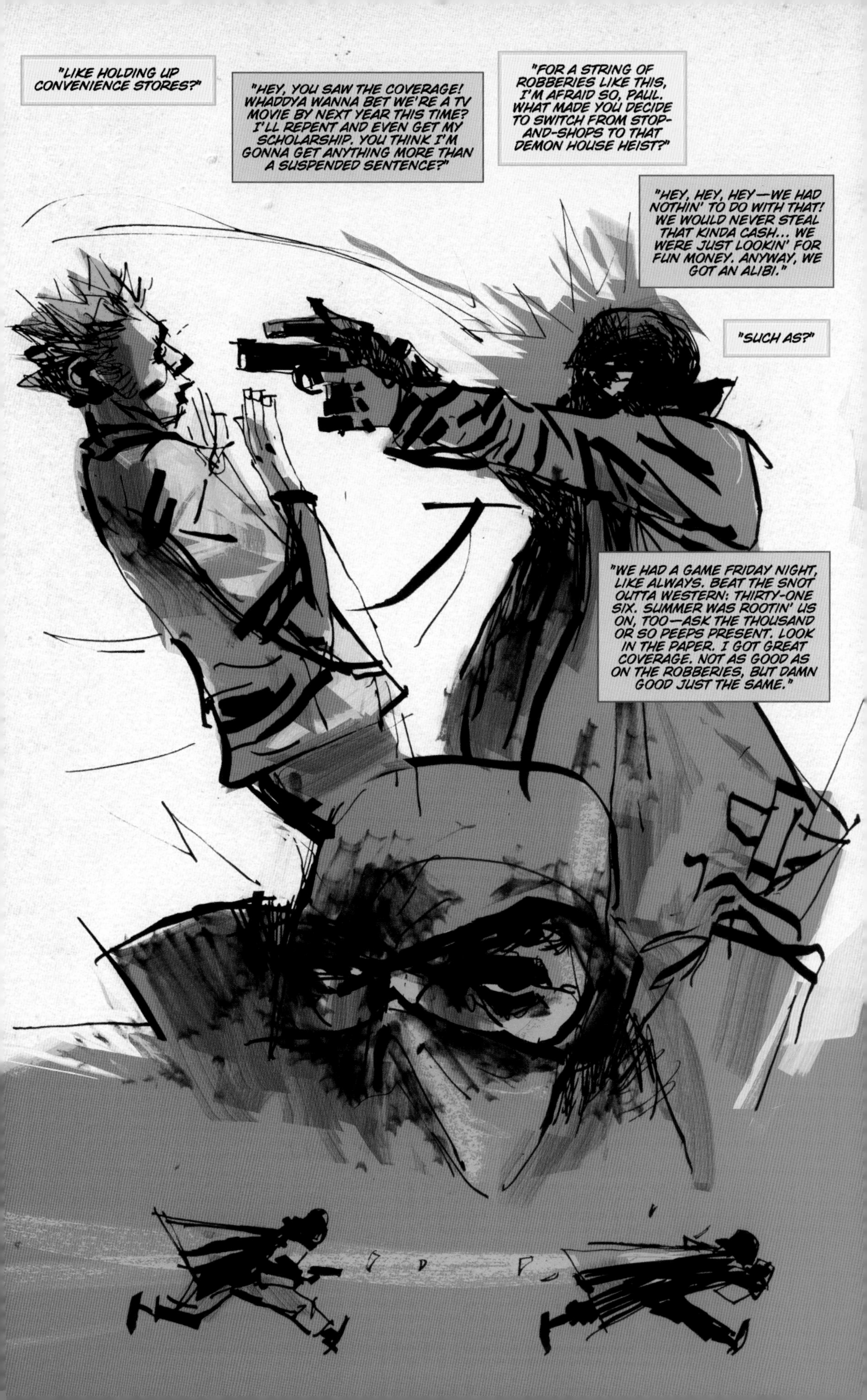
"LIKE HOLDING UP CONVENIENCE STORES?"
"HEY, YOU SAW THE COVERAGE! WHADDYA WANNA BET WE'RE A TV MOVIE BY NEXT YEAR THIS TIME? I'LL REPENT AND EVEN GET MY SCHOLARSHIP. YOU THINK I'M GONNA GET ANYTHING MORE THAN A SUSPENDED SENTENCE?"
"FOR A STRING OF ROBBERIES LIKE THIS, I'M AFRAID SO, PAUL. WHAT MADE YOU DECIDE TO SWITCH FROM STOP-AND-SHOPS TO THAT DEMON HOUSE HEIST?"
"HEY, HEY, HEY—WE HAD NOTHIN' TO DO WITH THAT! WE WOULD NEVER STEAL THAT KINDA CASH... WE WERE JUST LOOKIN' FOR FUN MONEY. ANYWAY, WE GOT AN ALIBI."
"SUCH AS?"
"WE HAD A GAME FRIDAY NIGHT, LIKE ALWAYS. BEAT THE SNOT OUTTA WESTERN: THIRTY-ONE SIX. SUMMER WAS ROOTIN' US ON, TOO—ASK THE THOUSAND OR SO PEEPS PRESENT. LOOK IN THE PAPER. I GOT GREAT COVERAGE. NOT AS GOOD AS ON THE ROBBERIES, BUT DAMN GOOD JUST THE SAME."

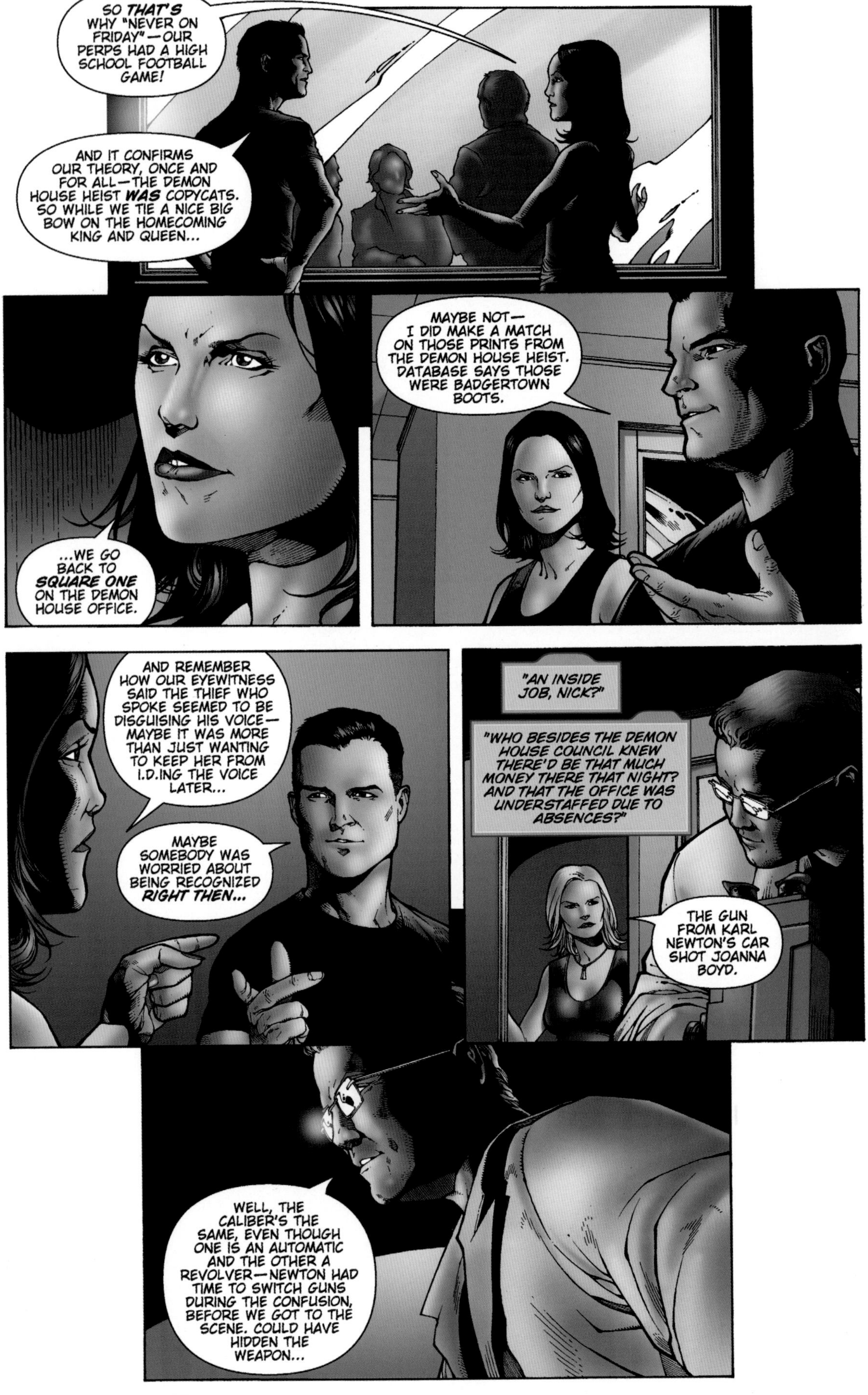
SO **THAT'S** WHY "NEVER ON FRIDAY"—OUR PERPS HAD A HIGH SCHOOL FOOTBALL GAME!
AND IT CONFIRMS OUR THEORY, ONCE AND FOR ALL—THE DEMON HOUSE HEIST **WAS** COPYCATS. SO WHILE WE TIE A NICE BIG BOW ON THE HOMECOMING KING AND QUEEN...
...WE GO BACK TO **SQUARE ONE** ON THE DEMON HOUSE OFFICE.
MAYBE NOT—I DID MAKE A MATCH ON THOSE PRINTS FROM THE DEMON HOUSE HEIST. DATABASE SAYS THOSE WERE BADGERTOWN BOOTS.
AND REMEMBER HOW OUR EYEWITNESS SAID THE THIEF WHO SPOKE SEEMED TO BE DISGUISING HIS VOICE—MAYBE IT WAS MORE THAN JUST WANTING TO KEEP HER FROM I.D.ING THE VOICE LATER...
MAYBE SOMEBODY WAS WORRIED ABOUT BEING RECOGNIZED **RIGHT THEN...**
"AN INSIDE JOB, NICK?"
"WHO BESIDES THE DEMON HOUSE COUNCIL KNEW THERE'D BE THAT MUCH MONEY THERE THAT NIGHT? AND THAT THE OFFICE WAS UNDERSTAFFED DUE TO ABSENCES?"
THE GUN FROM KARL NEWTON'S CAR SHOT JOANNA BOYD.
WELL, THE CALIBER'S THE SAME, EVEN THOUGH ONE IS AN AUTOMATIC AND THE OTHER A REVOLVER—NEWTON HAD TIME TO SWITCH GUNS DURING THE CONFUSION, BEFORE WE GOT TO THE SCENE. COULD HAVE HIDDEN THE WEAPON...

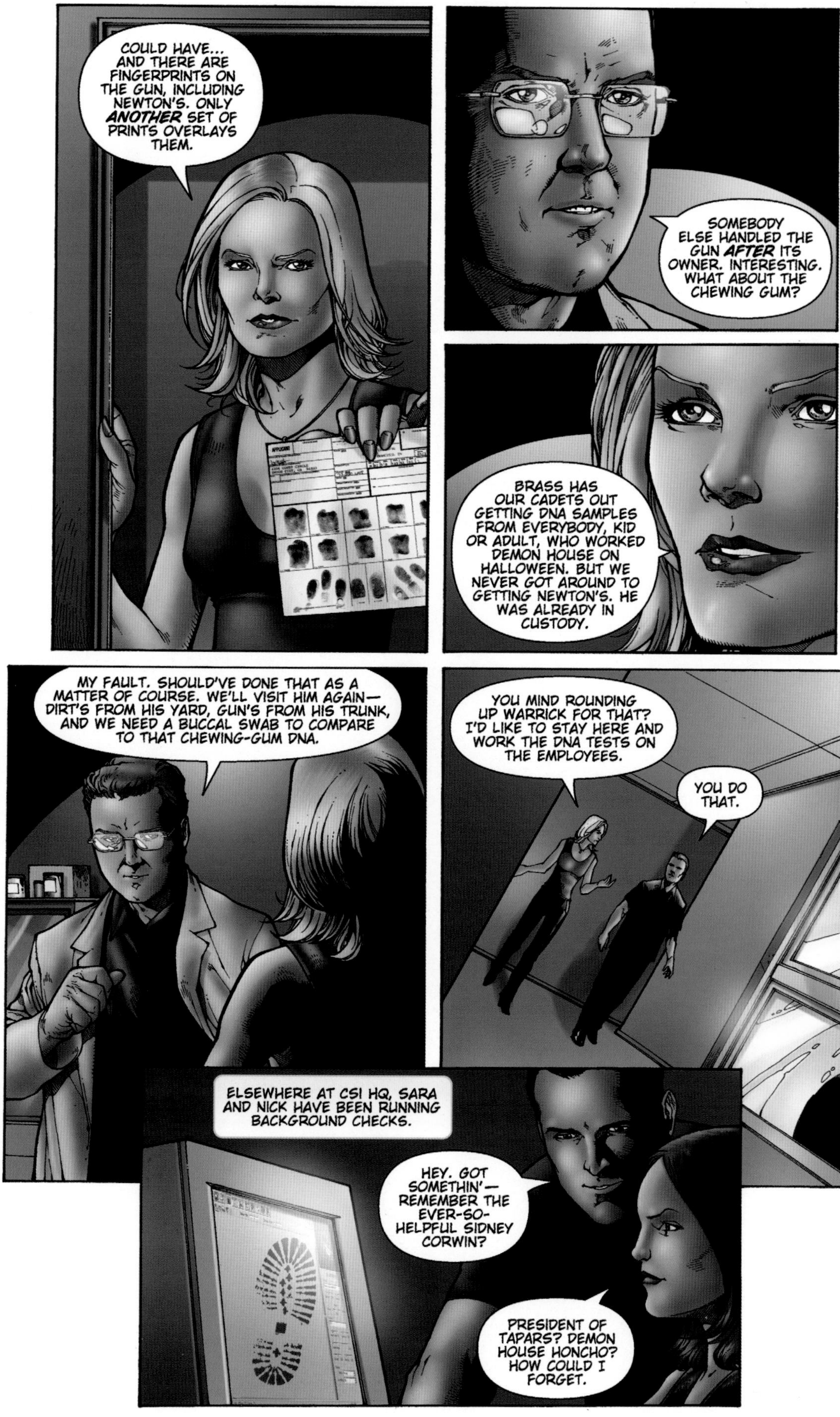
COULD HAVE... AND THERE ARE FINGERPRINTS ON THE GUN, INCLUDING NEWTON'S. ONLY ANOTHER SET OF PRINTS OVERLAYS THEM.
SOMEBODY ELSE HANDLED THE GUN AFTER ITS OWNER. INTERESTING. WHAT ABOUT THE CHEWING GUM?
BRASS HAS OUR CADETS OUT GETTING DNA SAMPLES FROM EVERYBODY, KID OR ADULT, WHO WORKED DEMON HOUSE ON HALLOWEEN. BUT WE NEVER GOT AROUND TO GETTING NEWTON'S. HE WAS ALREADY IN CUSTODY.
MY FAULT. SHOULD'VE DONE THAT AS A MATTER OF COURSE. WE'LL VISIT HIM AGAIN—DIRT'S FROM HIS YARD, GUN'S FROM HIS TRUNK, AND WE NEED A BUCCAL SWAB TO COMPARE TO THAT CHEWING-GUM DNA.
YOU MIND ROUNDING UP WARRICK FOR THAT? I'D LIKE TO STAY HERE AND WORK THE DNA TESTS ON THE EMPLOYEES.
YOU DO THAT.
ELSEWHERE AT CSI HQ, SARA AND NICK HAVE BEEN RUNNING BACKGROUND CHECKS.
HEY. GOT SOMETHIN'—REMEMBER THE EVER-SO-HELPFUL SIDNEY CORWIN?
PRESIDENT OF TAPARS? DEMON HOUSE HONCHO? HOW COULD I FORGET.

SEEMS HE'S BEEN MAKING SOME BAD CHOICES—LIKE GETTING INTO A LOAN SHARK FOR THIRTY LARGE.

GET OUT! *THAT* STRAIGHT-ARROW PIPSQUEAK?

YOU KNOW WHAT THEY SAY ABOUT STILL WATERS. AND ANYWAY, THAT LOAN SHARK'S NO PIPSQUEAK—FELLA NAMED MANNY TORQUEMUNDO, WHO BREAKS LEGS LIKE BUFFALO WINGS.

WHERE DID YOU GET THIS INFO, NICK?

I COULD PLAY MYSTERIOUS, LIKE I GOT SNITCHES OR SOMETHING... BUT THE TRUTH IS, O'RILEY WAS DOING SOME ROUTINE CROSS-REFERENCING WITH THE ORGANIZED CRIME UNIT AND MADE THE CONNECTION.

SARA, SEE IF YOU CAN RAISE BRASS ON YOUR CELL. WE SHOULDN'T GO CALLING ON MR. CORWIN WITHOUT A DETECTIVE ALONG.

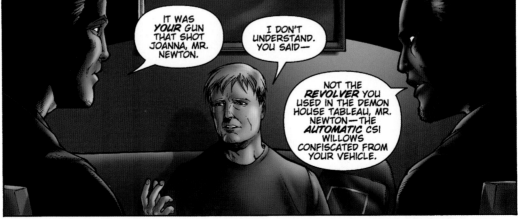

IT WAS *YOUR* GUN THAT SHOT JOANNA, MR. NEWTON.

I DON'T UNDERSTAND. YOU SAID—

NOT THE *REVOLVER* YOU USED IN THE DEMON HOUSE TABLEAU, MR. NEWTON—THE *AUTOMATIC* CSI WILLOWS CONFISCATED FROM YOUR VEHICLE.

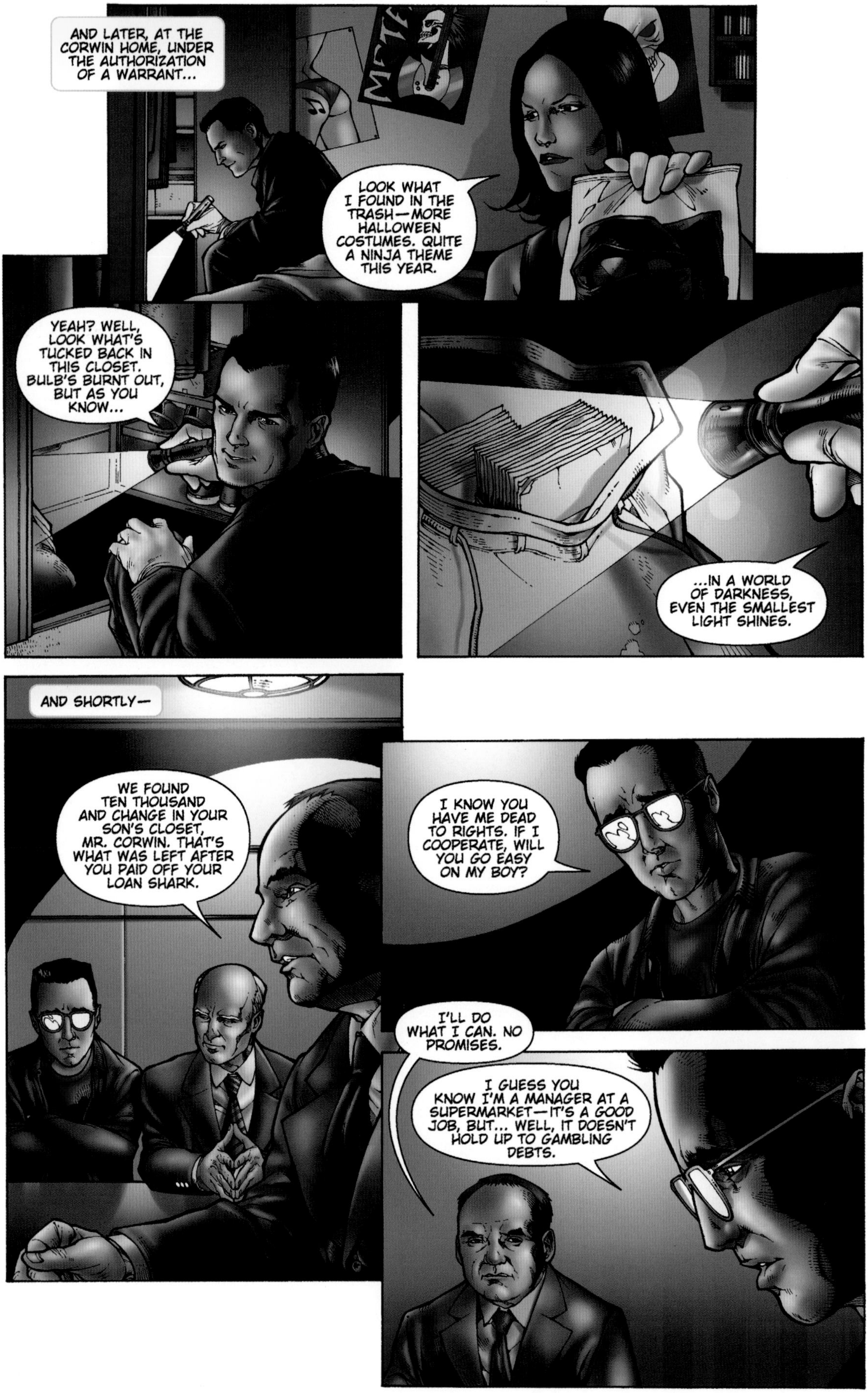
AND LATER, AT THE CORWIN HOME, UNDER THE AUTHORIZATION OF A WARRANT...
LOOK WHAT I FOUND IN THE TRASH—MORE HALLOWEEN COSTUMES. QUITE A NINJA THEME THIS YEAR.
YEAH? WELL, LOOK WHAT'S TUCKED BACK IN THIS CLOSET. BULB'S BURNT OUT, BUT AS YOU KNOW...
...IN A WORLD OF DARKNESS, EVEN THE SMALLEST LIGHT SHINES.
AND SHORTLY—
WE FOUND TEN THOUSAND AND CHANGE IN YOUR SON'S CLOSET, MR. CORWIN. THAT'S WHAT WAS LEFT AFTER YOU PAID OFF YOUR LOAN SHARK.
I KNOW YOU HAVE ME DEAD TO RIGHTS. IF I COOPERATE, WILL YOU GO EASY ON MY BOY?
I'LL DO WHAT I CAN. NO PROMISES.
I GUESS YOU KNOW I'M A MANAGER AT A SUPERMARKET—IT'S A GOOD JOB, BUT... WELL, IT DOESN'T HOLD UP TO GAMBLING DEBTS.

"MY WIFE RAN OFF AND LEFT US LAST YEAR, CAPTAIN BRASS. SHE MET HIM AT OUR CHURCH, CAN YOU BELIEVE THAT? SHE'D BEEN INSTRUMENTAL IN THE TAPARS WORK, TOO—WHAT A DAMN HYPOCRITE SHE TURNED OUT TO BE!

"THAT'S WHEN THE GAMBLING STARTED—I'D NEVER REALLY GONE TO THE CASINOS BEFORE, BUT I WAS TRYING TO FEEL BETTER, TO BE SUCCESSFUL AT SOMETHING. IT STARTED SMALL, AND I WON A LITTLE, GOT CONFIDENT, AND IT JUST KIND OF SPIRALED.

"MY SON WAS GOING TO JUNIOR COLLEGE, LOCALLY, BUT... WELL, HE FLUNKED OUT. I THINK HE WAS HIT PRETTY HARD WHEN HIS MOM LEFT US. WE TALKED ABOUT A NEW START FOR BOTH OF US. I GAVE UP GAMBLING... HAVEN'T SET FOOT IN A CASINO IN WEEKS. AND WE HAD A TRADE SCHOOL PICKED OUT FOR SID JR.

"BUT MY WIFE HAD CLEANED OUT OUR SAVINGS BEFORE SHE WENT, AND I WAS IN TO THAT SHARK. I HAD TO GET OUT FROM UNDER! AND I WANTED SID JR. TO HAVE A NEW START—TUITION MONEY, Y'KNOW?

"I ASKED THE TAPARS BOARD IF THEY COULD PUT ME ON SALARY... I'VE GIVEN HOUR UPON HOUR TO THE ORGANIZATION OVER THE YEARS. BUT THEY SAID NO. I MADE THEM HUNDREDS OF THOUSANDS OF DOLLARS. I FELT WE HAD A RIGHT TO TAKE A LITTLE OF IT BACK."

WE'VE GOT A RED FLAG ON ONE OF THE DNA TESTS FROM A KID WHO WORKED DEMON HOUSE THE NIGHT OF THE SHOOTING: RUTH NEWTON.

NEWTON'S *DAUGHTER?* SHE'S OUR SHOOTER?

NO. BUT HER DNA SHOWS THAT SHE'S RELATED TO OUR BUBBLE-GUM CHEWER, *AND* PROBABLE KILLER: HER BROTHER MARK.

JUST GOT OFF THE PHONE WITH TWO OF THEM—BOTH KIDS SAID THEY LOST TRACK OF MARK AROUND FIFTEEN MINUTES PRIOR TO THE STAMPEDE OUTTA DEMON HOUSE.

WHAT? WASN'T HE WITH HIS FRIENDS THAT NIGHT?

BRASS IS INTERVIEWING OUR "DEMON" GIRL, JAN TEMPLETON—YOU'RE GONNA WANT TO HEAR THIS, GRIS. TURNS OUT SHE'S MARK NEWTON'S BEST FRIEND'S GIRL...

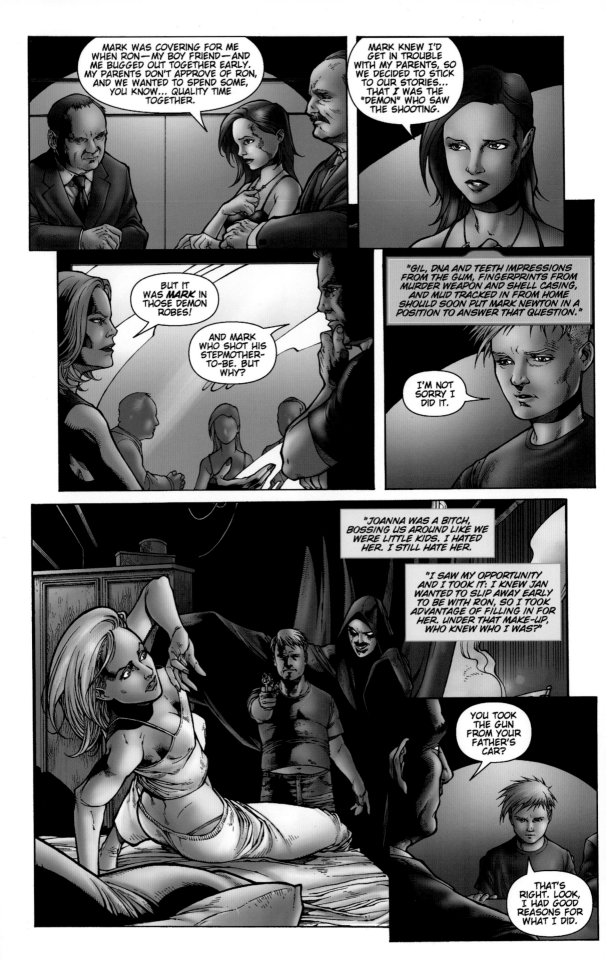

MARK WAS COVERING FOR ME WHEN RON—MY BOY FRIEND—AND ME BUGGED OUT TOGETHER EARLY. MY PARENTS DON'T APPROVE OF RON, AND WE WANTED TO SPEND SOME, YOU KNOW... QUALITY TIME TOGETHER.

MARK KNEW I'D GET IN TROUBLE WITH MY PARENTS, SO WE DECIDED TO STICK TO OUR STORIES... THAT *I* WAS THE "DEMON" WHO SAW THE SHOOTING.

BUT IT WAS *MARK* IN THOSE DEMON ROBES!

AND MARK WHO SHOT HIS STEPMOTHER-TO-BE. BUT WHY?

"GIL, DNA AND TEETH IMPRESSIONS FROM THE GUM, FINGERPRINTS FROM MURDER WEAPON AND SHELL CASING, AND MUD TRACKED IN FROM HOME SHOULD SOON PUT MARK NEWTON IN A POSITION TO ANSWER THAT QUESTION."

I'M NOT SORRY I DID IT.

"JOANNA WAS A BITCH, BOSSING US AROUND LIKE WE WERE LITTLE KIDS. I HATED HER. I STILL HATE HER.

"I SAW MY OPPORTUNITY AND I TOOK IT: I KNEW JAN WANTED TO SLIP AWAY EARLY TO BE WITH RON, SO I TOOK ADVANTAGE OF FILLING IN FOR HER. UNDER THAT MAKE-UP, WHO KNEW WHO I WAS?"

YOU TOOK THE GUN FROM YOUR FATHER'S CAR?

THAT'S RIGHT. LOOK, I HAD GOOD REASONS FOR WHAT I DID.

Books of interest from IDW Publishing

CSI: Demon House
Max Allan Collins
Gabriel Rodriguez/Ashley Wood
124 pages • $19.99
ISBN: 1-932382-34-8

CSI: Serial
Max Allan Collins
Gabriel Rodriguez/Ashley Wood
144 pages • $19.99
ISBN: 1-932382-02-X

The Shield: Spotlight
Jeff Mariotte
Jean Diaz/Tommy Lee Edwards
128 pages • $19.99
ISBN: 1-932382-23-2

Will Eisner's John Law
Will Eisner/Gary Chaloner
80 pages • $14.99
ISBN: 1-932382-27-5

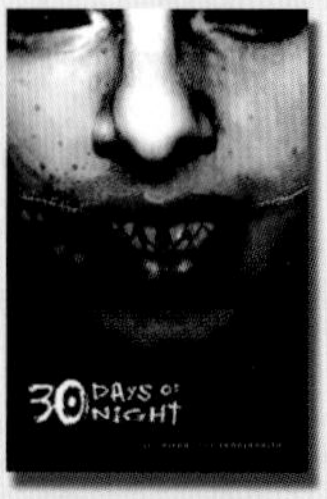

30 Days of Night
Steve Niles/Ben Templesmith
104 pages • $17.99
ISBN: 0-9719775-5-0

Dark Days
Steve Niles/Ben Templesmith
144 pages • $19.99
ISBN: 1-932382-16-X

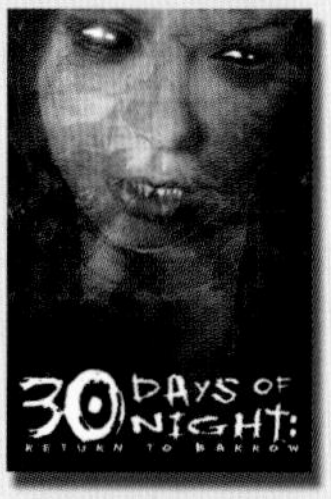

**30 Days of Night:
Return to Barrow**
Steve Niles/Ben Templesmith
144 pages • $19.99
ISBN: 1-932382-36-4

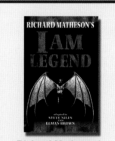

**Richard Matheson's
I Am Legend**
adapted by Steve Niles/Elman Brown
248 pages • HC • $35.00
ISBN: 1-932382-08-9

George A. Romero's
Dawn of the Dead
Steve Niles/Chee
104 pages • $17.99
ISBN: 1-932382-32-1

Wake the Dead
Steve Niles/Chee
128 pages • $19.99
ISBN: 1-932382-22-4

Aleister Arcane
Steve Niles/Breehn Burns
104 pages • $17.99
ISBN: 1-932382-33-X

IDW's Tales of Terror
Various
96 pages • HC • $16.99
ISBN: 1-932382-31-3

Silent Hill: Dying Inside
Scott Ciencin/Ben Templesmith
Aadi Salman/Ashley Wood
128 pages • $19.99
ISBN: 1-932382-24-0

Underworld
Kris Oprisko/Danny McBride
Nick Postic/Nick Marinkovich
144 pages • $19.99
ISBN: 1-932382-26-7

CVO
Alex Garner/Jeff Mariotte
Mindy Lee/Gabriel Hernandez
116 pages • $19.99
ISBN: 1-932382-40-2

**Popbot Collection
Book Two**
Ashley Wood
154 pages • $35.00
ISBN: 1-932382-52-6

www.**idwpublishing**.com